# Salvador Sabino
# Two Ways

## Washington Heights Drug Dealer Turns Around

EBED PRESS
NEW YORK

*Two Ways*
*by Salvador Sabino*
*Second Printing March 2004*

Copyright ©2003 by Ebed Press, Inc
3103 Villa Ave., New York, NY, 10468, USA
www.ebedpress.com


ISBN: 0-9741927-0-8

Also available in the Spanish language under the title:
*Dos Caminos by Salvador Sabino*
Published by Editorial Vida ©2002
Miami, Florida 33166-4665

Cover design by:
Mariel Alvarez
www.thestorecompany.com
Brooklyn, New York

*Printed in the United States of America*

# Contents

Introduction......................................................5

Chapter1 Seasons............................................7

Chapter 2 Origins............................................19

Chapter 3 Skyscrapers......................................27

Chapter 4 Changes...........................................41

Chapter 5 Streets.............................................47

Chapter 6 Sales...............................................53

Chapter 7 Addictions........................................61

Chapter 8 Connections.....................................75

Chapter 9 Robberies.........................................83

Chapter 10 Arrests...........................................95

Chapter 11 Behind Bars....................................111

Chapter 12 Options..........................................135

Chapter 13 Encounters.....................................149

Chapter 14 Commisions....................................167

Chapter 15 Souls.............................................183

Chapter 16 Mighty Acts....................................209

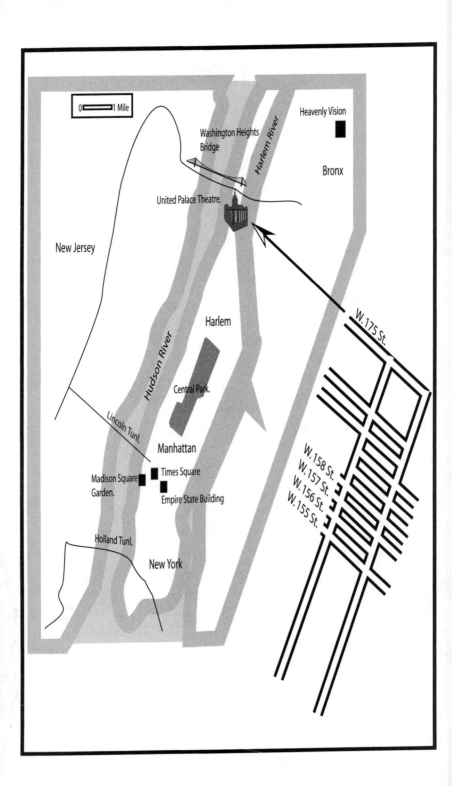

# Introduction

"Broad is the way that leads to destruction and there are many who go in by it. Because narrow is the gate and difficult is the way which leads to life and there are few who find it." —Jesus in Matthew 7:13 and 14 (NKJV)

In the streets of Manhattan's Washington Heights, beautiful turn of the century architecture along broad avenues anchored misery, filth and desperation down most of its side streets. In the late 70s and early 80s, Black and Latino gangs competed for territory and drug clientele. Sal Sabino mastered the drug trade — until drugs mastered him.

As a boy he had longed to be a baseball player, as a youth, a musician. There were some over the course of his young life who said he had a call to preach.

But a series of choices fed by a root of bitterness and violence led him first to seeming heights as a wealthy and powerful drug dealer, then to depths as a convict and drug addict... until he made the decisive choice.

New York City was just getting to know itself again after nearly two decades of peace protests, transit and garbage strikes, and a budget catastrophe that left its finances in the control of a board of watchdogs outside the city government. Prosperity and stability were inching back in. But the Big Apple still had a notorious crime rate, and a reputation for filth and violence to go along with its fame as a center for art and commerce. It's no surprise, then, that it was a patchwork of posh and impoverished neighborhoods.

Washington Heights — just north of Harlem and just over the George Washington Bridge from New Jersey — was a bi-cultural mix of beauty and squalor. Spanish — mostly Dominican accented — and English wove together in the airwaves. In summertime, salsa and in later years, merengue, enhanced the soundtrack of street life in the

Heights. Young men and women, coiffed and colorful in the latest fashions and hairstyles emerged from doorways of broken down buildings. As night came on, rats and roaches scurried about in a search for food and the next hiding place.

Vermin stayed out of the headquarters of the most successful drug dealers — who occupied spaces in the better — kept buildings and made sure their apartments were done up executive style with only the best furnishings.

Everywhere the aroma of cuchifrito — favorite fried foods like pastelitos, empanadas and chicken — enticed the working people, street hustlers, small business people, big drug dealers, seniors and children who all shared this neighborhood.

The people of the Heights also shared the smell of death — premature and violent death. Candles alongside makeshift altars built around pictures of the various personalities from the occult religion Santeria memorialized those killed in fights for turf, drugs or revenge. The Rivera Funeral Home at 173rd Street and St. Nicholas Avenue did a steady business in transporting the bodies of young men back to the Dominican Republic for burial.

Death was a common theme in colorful murals or simpler graffiti on the sides of commercial or public buildings.

Today Washington Heights — along with many parts of the city — has changed. Fewer aimless young people are seen just hanging out. More businesses are moving into the area. Better police presence and more sophisticated security have added stability. Crime has decreased and programs for youth have increased. More churches are opening now than ever before and the message of Jesus Christ is no longer seen as something just for old people, but for all people.

The amazing transformation in the life of Sal Sabino is a mini-portrait of the Holy Spirit at work in the city that never sleeps, the city God watches over 24 hours a day, the city He loves so much. These pages contain that story which, at the start of this new millennium, is still unfolding.

# 1
# SEASONS

The clock struck midnight. With every passing minute, every passing second, the hour drew nearer. Well, my grandmother had said, you reap what you sow.

Just past my 23rd birthday, I found myself in the Corzo Night Club, surrounded by couples happily streaming onto the dance floor and other partiers huddling around the band just enjoying the music. Trumpets blared and drumbeats ricocheted, but all I felt was misery. I tried to fight it off with heavy doses of liquor and cocaine but the dose of worry I was drinking was stronger than music or drugs.

It was New Year's Eve. The old man, as they say, had died and a new year was born. It was the start of a new decade. To many people it was the 80s, but for me it was the decade of imprisonment. My worry was facing the judge who had told me at my last court appearance in a stone cold voice: "Sentencing, January 3, 9 a.m." There was no way out. I had pled guilty.

I sat remembering how the co-worker of a childhood friend, Ruben, laid out to us the perfect plan, easily executed, for robbing more than seventy-five thousand dollars. That day, dressed in stylish executive suits, we walked right past the guards at the factory complex. We slipped behind a row of vans, opened our Samsonite briefcases and pulled out our disguises: a long black coat, gloves, a mask and finally, a revolver for each of us. We did not consider the possibility that it might rain nor that the paymaster would be unusually late. We lit one cigarette after another with the smoldering butt of the previous one as we waited. I had always enjoyed watching Ruben smoke. He would strike very theatrical poses when he lit up, especially when girls were around. Now, however, it was obvious that he was smoking, not for pleasure, but to calm his nerves. We had made our share of mischief in the past, running with our teenage friends. But this was different. We weren't just out shoplifting, smoking a bag of marijuana, going to a dance or a movie. We'd raised the stakes to feed our fantasies of expensive, late model cars and, more than that, "getting out of the barrio."

## Armed robbery

There behind the cargo vans, under the rain, we dreamed of getting a better way of life even at someone else's expense. I was sitting, smoking and daydreaming, and blowing smoke rings, when I noticed a sudden change in Ruben's demeanor. He didn't need to say anything. We knew each other. The moment had arrived. The man we were waiting for, the paymaster for five different businesses, opened the trunk of his car. Ruben startled him from behind; I jumped in front. "Alto ahi, don't move," I screamed.

When the man looked behind him and saw Ruben, he let out a fierce yell. Ruben tried to quiet him with a violent blow to the head with the butt of his revolver. I ran to the trunk of the car, looking for the money. I took out a manila envelope but was interrupted by two men running toward us, revolvers drawn. Ruben took something in his hand and signaled me to get out of there. Then he started running toward the car while I held off the two men with my gun. At this point, they were trying desperately to calm the paymaster who had gone into hysterics as blood poured from his forehead.

"Anyone who wants to die — follow us or call the police," I threatened, covering Ruben while moving toward the car.

As soon as we got in the vehicle, guns in hand, Zebra, who we had hired under the guise of needing a ride to do business in New Jersey, was alarmed.

"What happened, loco? What happened?!," he screamed.

"Hurry up," we ordered him. The tires squealed as he peeled out of the complex.

"What did you do?" demanded Hilda, staring at her husband. Meanwhile, Ruben caressed his four-month-old son Napoleon.

"Nothing," he lied.

# Checkmate on Route 3 East

As soon as we got onto Route 3, headed for the Lincoln Tunnel and New York City, we started looking for an alternate route, because we knew the tunnel was under tight surveillance. Then I noticed a truck following us at a distance. I had seen it near the crime scene. Zebra sped up until it was out of sight. Minutes later, a police car pulled up behind us but, since the siren wasn't going, we kept on driving. Then it was joined by three other patrol cars, one behind, one alongside and finally, one that pulled in front of us. We shoved everything into one of the briefcases while I tried to figure out a way to get rid of all the evidence. But it was too late. The sirens went off. The police yelled through bullhorns: "Stop! Pull over to the right."

We stopped. There was no other choice. They had us in checkmate. Police got out on all sides with revolvers and rifles drawn.

"Put your hands up or we'll fire," yelled the agents.

Back at the precinct, Ruben and I declared our own guilt so that Zebra, Hilda and baby Napoleon could go free. They weren't guilty at all. They didn't even know we were wanted for assault until they heard the formal charges, with bail set at $50,000 for Ruben and for me.

Even though we tried to convince the police of Zebra's innocence, they didn't let him go right away, because there apparently was a warrant for his arrest in New York. He had to make bail of $25,000. Since I had invited him to the supposed financial transaction, they had to put us in separate cells to keep us from fighting.

Days later, my path to perdition led me behind the iron bars of the Hudson County Jail in Jersey City, New Jersey, thinking I should have shot down the police who arrested me. The jailer's voice interrupted my thoughts.

"Salvador Sabino, you have a visitor," he told me.

When my cell door opened, I expected to see my lawyer but it was my uncle, Pastor Antonio Jimenez. He came with the same message as always, undaunted by my new residence. He raised his right hand, gestured wildly with two of his fingers and held his Bible in the other hand.

"In life, there are two ways," he called out. It was his favorite theme — the narrow way that leads to life and the broad way that leads to destruction. It was embarrassing, especially with the other inmates looking on. We were all flabbergasted by his thundering declaration. Turning back into my cell, I thought: "He's just like every other Bible thumper — stark raving mad."

I got out on bail and continued in the way that would

lead to destruction. Stuck in that lifestyle, I wasn't interested in changing. My desires for women, drugs and nightclubs had me trapped like a bug in the sticky fibers of a spider's web. Though I did not belong to a band, I loved going to clubs and discotheques almost every day of the week. I didn't dance. I preferred to sit at a table with friends drinking cognac, which I combined with two or three marijuana cigarettes and hits of cocaine.

I had planned to avoid sentencing through a pre-trial intervention program, but during one of the sessions, the counselor surprised me by grabbing my right hand and pointing out that my thumb and index finger were yellowed. It was evidence of my constant marijuana habit. She was alarmed!

"Mr. Sabino. What's this?" she asked without hiding her anger. I was immediately expelled from the program and consequently referred for sentencing.

## Pre-court jitters

I couldn't enjoy myself in the bar that night. A few minutes after midnight, I started counting the hours until I would have to go before the judge for sentencing. "How many years will I have to be in prison? What a miserable trap I stepped into. I'll be just like all the others. My friends will forget me. My girlfriends won't love me anymore. I'm ruined." The voice of Ruben's mother-in-law, Quintana, echoed in my mind: "I'll make sure your sons read this article," she had threatened as she shoved a copy of "El Diario La Prensa," the city's Spanish language newspaper, in his face. We'd made the front page on Sept. 25, 1978.

My girlfriend abruptly stopped the stream of gloomy thoughts. "Sal, what happened to you? Everybody's dancing. Everybody's having a good time. And you're sitting here looking so bitter and depressed. You're not thinking of someone else, are you?" she questioned me.

I said nothing but sat watching the dancers turning to the rhythms pulsing from Luis Perico Ortiz and his orchestra. "De patita el perro con la gatita," went the song. A long drag on my cigarette, another shot of cognac, then another hit of cocaine. Finally, I answered her coldly, "I'm leaving New York. I don't know when I'll be back."

Solomon the sage said: "There is a time for everything, and a season for every activity under heaven."(Ecclesiastes 3:1) As I was getting dressed for court the next day, I didn't want to see anyone, especially not my mother. What audacity it would take to face the woman whose dreams today were going up in smoke! All her life as a mother she had sacrificed to make a way for her only son. The dream of seeing him become a doctor, lawyer or engineer had become the burden of seeing him indicted for armed robbery, sentenced and thrown into the penitentiary. I approached her room.

"Juanita, calm down. You'll hurt yourself crying so much. At least your son is alive," said my stepfather, Delfin, trying to console her.

I could toughen myself up for a fight with the most dangerous, most notorious thugs. I would go hand-to-hand with guys better armed than me. But I didn't have the guts to look at the face of the woman crying tears of blood, the one who had denied herself all her life just so that now her only son could deceive her so badly. I left the apartment and headed to court without saying anything to her.

Finally, the moment came: "All rise," intoned the bailiff as the judge entered the room. For the court, I was just one more case. But this was the darkest day of my life. A guy who had always been surrounded by lots friends, I now stood completely alone. Not even Ruben, who was due to receive his sentence, was in court. The bang of the gavel got everyone's attention. My attorney John Dwire approached to offer me consolation. The guards also approached.

# The start of a new life

I heard the sound of the handcuffs and I could see out of the corner of my eye one of the guards getting ready to put them on me. The judge pronounced sentence: concurrent indeterminate sentence of three and five years. He banged the gavel and I was cuffed and taken through a tunnel. At the end, they took off the handcuffs. They handed me a pillow rolled inside some sheets. A door of iron bars was opened and shut behind me. I immediately threw the pillow onto my new bed and went to the telephone. Someone was already using it, talking very calmly.

" Listen, I have to make an emergency call. You're taking too much time," I yelled at the person on the phone.

He looked me up and down and put his hand over the receiver.

"I'll talk however long I want," he answered. But he quickly wrapped up the conversation and hung up.

I called my stepfather to let him know about the sentence. I asked about my mother and he told me she still had not stopped crying. While I was still talking, I noticed that the man who had been using the phone before me seemed to be getting ready to fight me. I said goodbye to my stepfather, asking him to console my mother and telling him that my attorney had assured me that I would not spend more than one year in jail. Then I went to my cell, took off my suit and tie and left. An experienced prisoner that they called Indio, who was also from New York, came up to me and offered some advice.

"I guess you're from New York. Take it easy, if you don't want a hassle every day. Learn to take your time," he warned me.

At that moment, the man who had been talking on the phone earlier came up to both of us and pointed at me with his right index finger.

"What's your problem?" he challenged me.

"Hold on," Indio intervened. "You guys are Latinos and while I'm around, all Latinos have to treat each other like brothers."

Minutes later, someone told me another prisoner from New York had arrived. It was my friend Ruben.

"Sal, this is tough. Who's going to take care of my wife and my little boy?" Ruben cried.

"Don't think about it so much," I answered sharply.

He began to act differently. He was listless; he was saying strange things. It looked to me like prison life and his worries were going to drive him crazy. There were a lot of people who lost the ability to think and act clearly under the pressures of prison life.

## Prison riot

I learned quickly that in the prisons there existed gangs of every kind: organized by race, nationality, region and also by religion. In the penitentiary at Bordentown, New Jersey, — which in 1980 was mainly a juvenile correctional facility — about six months after I arrived, there was a race riot during which the blacks really gave it to the whites. Gino, the leader of the small group of white prisoners, came to me and asked for the help of the Latino group.

We concluded that the problem was racial; therefore, we decided not to give Gino the weapons he asked for, much less fight in favor of his gang, though we didn't think the blacks were right either. Of all the whites, Gino had earned the hatred of the opposing gang because among the many tattoos he had on his body — so many he resembled a newspaper — the one covering his left arm was a picture of a black man hung from a tree. Gino, understanding that he had not won over the Latinos, became enraged and lashed out against the nearest black man. Immediately, convicts from both groups faced off in violent combat. Minutes later, prison officials showed up and began beating, kicking and shoving to try and break up the riot. Two or three of the guards tried to separate Gino and his victim, who was screaming in anguish. "Get him off me, he's biting me. Get him off me!" he yelled.

While the police were separating them, blood was running all over the tattoos on Gino's chest. Then, with his mouth full of blood, he spit out a piece of the left ear of his enemy, while letting out a fierce victory cry. Gino had been known by the nickname "Wild Man," — due to his long, unkempt red hair, his luxuriant beard and reputation as a biker gang member. Now, he'd really earned it. The few whites, including those who'd taken part in the racial attack, had to be moved to another section of the penitentiary. The most violent were moved to another prison.

On one occasion, when members of the different groups were just relaxing and watching television, another inmate swaggered in, changed the channel and sat down defiantly. I switched the channel back, looked the aggressor in the eyes and warned him: "What do you think? You're at home. Touch that television again and I'll leave a knuckle print in your face."

# Inmates cooperate

The tension of the riots among the different ethnic and regional groups seemed to dominate the environment, as if race or where you were born or lived were more important than justice or right. When I was just a few months from release, they transferred me from my job inside the jail, where I was a butcher, to one outside. I had to work in the apple orchard in front of the prison. That gave us the opportunity to ask a friend to bring us a good supply of marijuana and cocaine, which he would put in a package under a fallen tree in the part of the orchard near the road used by visitors going into the main door of the prison. The orchard workers — white, black, Latino — worked in great harmony to make sure this deceit was successful. One detained the guard assigned to us, two more kept watch for the warden or other supervisors; the others kept working except for the one responsible for looking for the drugs. Then the package of drugs was distributed and we all had a good laugh over prison security and the way we had managed our triumphal entry.

We smoked marijuana almost every day. On special occasions, we had liquor, cocaine, heroin or a varied selection of pills. My friend Benny, also from New York, had spent almost his entire youth going from prison to prison and was extremely anxious unless he was under the influence of some kind of drug. But there was one day of the week the two of us had agreed to take off from hallucinogens. That was on Mondays, when the Pentecostals came to the chapel to sing the little worship choruses that, every once in a while, even brought us to tears.

On one occasion, I had a falling out with one of my coworkers over drugs. I grabbed a weapon, a homemade prison blade called a shank and told him: "Get your shank. I'll be waiting in the bathroom," I dared him.

The other prisoners scattered. Benny and another friend stood guard. Two men in their thirties, older than us, walked into the bathroom.

"Sabino, listen up, that boy doesn't want any trouble with you. He's ready to cop out," one said.

"Dominican, you get mad over every little thing. Everybody around here likes you. We're a family. Don't be so violent," added the other.

The following day, things were still tense. In the dining room, the seasoned prisoners came up to me and told me that if I didn't change my attitude, I would never get out of prison. Serapio, an inmate from Puerto Rico, the oldest of all of us, approached me. "You're very lucky to be alive. You were born with an angel that protects you. God protected you the other day when you ran up to the gym teacher and tried to kick him. Just for that, they could have given you two more years in jail. I think there's only one thing that can save you," he advised me. "You've got to turn to Christ."

# 2
# ORIGINS

Why did I behave that way? What was the source, the root of this violence? I was born in the Dominican Republic in Ingenio Angelina de San Pedro de Macorís. Out of my distant memories, I remember hearing my grandmother say: "Every child crawls, uses a pacifier, and then walks. However, my first grandchild never crawled or used a pacifier and, as soon he could stand up, he ran as fast as he could, as if flying were the next thing to do." Many times over I heard my relatives say humorously, yet in a tone of concern: "This kid is going to turn into a mobster. As soon as he turns fifteen, he will be unbearable, and end up in prison."

As a child, I loved to play with toys. My favorite holiday was "Three Kings Day"— a Christmas festivity in which children whose parents can buy them gifts, get presents. In the Caribbean, on the eve of this much anticipated day, children put grass and a glass of water under their bed, supposedly for the king's camels to eat and drink. They want to win the kings' favor and, in exchange, receive the toys they requested.

What disappointment my friend Tetelo and his three brothers suffered every year! As soon as they woke up in the morning, they would thrust themselves under the bed to see what they had received, and as always, the kings had brought them a khaki colored school uniform. "Those kings are no good. They only bring toys to certain kids, and none for me, Tetelo would say.

For him, his three brothers and many other children, Three Kings' Day was a nightmare; to me, it was the best day on the calendar. It was my favorite. The sounds of trains, cars, whistles, flutes, bugles, and the lights and colors of the toys just fascinated me. But the toys I would often ask the kings for were pistols, rifles and machine guns. In addition, the kings were so nice to me that not only did they leave toys at my grandmother's house, with whom I lived, but they would also deliver some to my father's house and my godmother's house too. At least, that's what I thought.

## Grandfather: Violent role model

My grandfather, Abigail Jimenez, was very loving with me. I heard him say many times: "Of all the family, you are the spitting image of me and that's why I have decided that you will be my heir. I'm surrounded by crows, just as the adage says: 'He has brought up a crow to pick out his own eyes.' You and your mother Juanita resemble my mother; so you are my only relatives: the rest are all crows." Then he would take out his comb, wrapped in a piece of wax paper, and begin playing, just like a harmonica, the melody of his favorite meringue: "Juanita Morel, oye tu merengue. Entre las mujeres, tu eres mi derriengue. Lelolai lelola"

He would often walk with me, taking me by the hand, and teaching me what life was about, so that, as he said, "no one can put fairytales into your head." One day there were lots of people outside the big huts where we lived—where most of the low-income people, such as the sugar cane farmers, lived. We were walking hand in hand, when suddenly his expression changed to a frown. He let go of my hand and commanded: "Go home quickly, go!" He frightened me badly. I could smell danger. And, at age five, I already recognized the signs of a fight brewing. My grandfather behaved like the "skells" that I would see going for their machetes in the sugar factory of Angelina. I ran, but not toward the house of Tata—my grandmother. Instead I hid under the big huts. These were large dwellings built on solid pillars of wood. I was lying underneath the huts, terrified, when I saw my grandfather. I heard him say: "Your hour has come; come so you can die like a man." My small body was trembling and, crying desperately, I could see through my tears my grandfather take a long knife and stab his opponent to death. Men who had been resting under the trees sharpening their machetes, hoes and sickles, jumped to their feet, agitated and shouting... The country guards came on horseback, firing shots into the air. My grandfather was arrested. The dead man was taken to the cemetery in a Haitian ceremony where men carry the simple wood coffin over their shoulders and chant back and forth: "Mampote. Uh, uh.Mampote. Uh, uh." In deeply emotional dialogue, with a mixture of joy and pain, the participants say "Mampote", which means: "I take you", then take two steps toward the cemetery. The others answer: "Uh, Uh", which means "No, no", then take a step back, portraying the idea that the dead person does not want to be buried.

## Witness to another stabbing

I'm not sure how long after this I experienced the second violent incident, although I'm certain that I was no more than six years old. I saw a young man run into a neighbor's house, furiously grab a knife and run back out into the street. I heard the fighting. And when I managed to get outside, in front of the house, I saw the first youth locked in gory combat with another. Both fell to the ground in the middle of the street and, as they insulted each other, exchanging obscene words, the first youth took out the knife and began stabbing the second one, who tried several times to get back up, but kept bleeding and falling to the ground. He screamed and writhed in pain, until he died.

A psychoanalyst would probably find in these experiences the roots of my criminal instinct. I heard many people, even in my own family say of me: "That boy, one of these days, will need to go to a correctional institution."

From a young age, in school, at the amusement parks, and in my own home, I would fist fight, and sometimes use simple things as weapons against other children. I was very friendly on one hand, but on the other I was very dangerous.

As my process of socialization advanced and I grew, we moved into different neighborhoods in San Pedro de Macoris. Our semi-nomadic journey ended in the neighborhood of Restauracion.

# Home life

In a house made of palm and wood, maybe the third house built in this new neighborhood, lived my grandmother with her husband Rafael, whom I called papa; my aunt Margarita; my uncle Bartolo, his wife and their three children; and the uninvited guests that would come by donkey, horse, or car, arriving mostly from the fields where the Jimenez family came from. This must have been the reason why our neighbors in Ingenio Angelina christened this branch of my family "los muchos" (the many). This side of my family had the ability to multiply and set up ten people to live under a roof made for three. My cousins and I would start fighting before even washing our faces in the morning, all the way into the night when we washed our feet before bed. Our fights were daily, but no one could split us apart. We would hang out and play together. Although we always fought, if someone apart from our family would come against one of us, they were in for a great surprise. Without even checking if it was right or wrong, we would gang up on them. One would throw a stone, the other would beat the guy with a stick, and whoever had a chance would sink his teeth into the victim.

Tetelo's parents also emigrated from Angelina to the Restauracion neighborhood. He was two years older than I, and was the first one to stand up for me. In a short time we became the leaders of a small gang that was mischievous and fought against the youth of other neighborhoods. Nobody would dare go to the Guazuma, a tree that was on the corner of the neighborhood's bodega, our hangout spot. One time, one of our most dangerous rivals came along with others from his neighborhood and a big fight broke out with stones and sticks that made the neighbors despise us; "Those guys, those tigers, need to be sent to prison before they kill one of us."

I'm sure my father knew very little about me. My behavior was quite different when I spent a few days with him and my brothers. Apart from that, papa Rafael and my uncle Bartolo had to work to support their families. My mother began traveling to Puerto Rico, seeking a better life. I was practically on my own; I was a "lawless goat." During fourth grade I was suspended from a Christian school because during the prayer time I would take advantage of the fact that the rest of my classmates had their eyes closed; I would bop them on the head and then quickly pretend I was praying.

## Suicide in the home

As I grew up I saw one tragedy after another. This was fostering violence in me. One morning, we were all on the patio of our home having our breakfast of bread and coffee, and papa Rafael walked up and spoke to my little cousin Altagracia. She suffered from chronic rheumatism that caused her such extreme painthat she would yell loudly enough to be heard throughout the neighborhood. Papa used to give her five cents a day. What he said to her that morning would forever remain in my memory:

—Take these five cents. I'll never be able to give them to you again.

My grandmother Tata came up and asked with much concern:

—Why do you say that, Rafael Sosa?

He was silent. We had to work hard to get a word out of him But my grandmother's insistence matched the intensity of his silence. —What are you saying Rafael?

From the youngest to the oldest, we were all paying attention.
—You will never see me again. I've just poisoned myself, —he cried out with much grief.
We all embraced him and began shouting.
—Rafael, what have you done? What have you done? My grandmother exclaimed repeatedly in agony.

At about 11a.m., with the house full of people, came the bad news: "Rafael is dead", said Abelino, a neighbor who had just ridden his bicycle from the hospital. The screaming got louder as Nerola arrived. She was supposedly so connected with the "spirit world", that there wasn't a mystery that she couldn't unveil.
"Rafael did not poison himself because of debt, as they are saying. He was killed by an expert piece of witchcraft," said Nerola. She promised to show us the face of the person who had sold Rafael to the spirits.She chose ten men from the family, took a glass full of water, and directed the men to form a circle around her. I heard someone say: "I suspected it was Tiriton, the Haitian. He will die the same death."
Instantly, everybody reacted and began making threats. A lady had a nervous breakdown: "Let me see that

killer!" she yelled hysterically. But the sorceress firmly challenged us with her metallic voice: "Whoever tries to approach, I will cast to the ground so that he or she may learn to respect the mysteries."

For my part, I loved papa Rafael very much. But I had seen so many movies of "bandidos" and cowboys that I believed that loving him also meant it would be my duty to avenge his death when I grew up. With this in mind, I hurled myself into the circle of men preventing me from seeing the face of the supposed assassin; but I stumbled, fell to the ground and sensed that everyone was looking down at me.

The witch approached me with the glass of water in one hand. With the other hand, she pointed at me and said in the cold, hard voice that I detested: "This boy needs to be protected or he will die with his boots on."

## Violence and injustice

Some time later, two youths older than I were fighting. They were about 15 years old. In the big cities, country people are usually ridiculed. But this time, the country boy was ridiculing his opponent, in front of everyone, across from La Guazuma. The rest were making fun of the way the country boy was giving the other a lesson in boxing. After the fight was over, the shamefaced father of the boy who was beat up arrived at La Guazuma with a police officer. The country boy's father arrived some minutes later and the police officer asked him to hand over his knife. He resisted. The police officer got very angry and, taking his gun out and yelling, said: "Let go of the knife or I'll shoot, you stupid old man."

At that time, a second police officer arrived. Without hesitation — though the country boy's father was under control and 15 feet away — the officer pulled the trigger

and shot the man in the abdomen. The old man began wob-
bling and fell to the ground. The people began protesting
such a cruel act of barbarism. At that point, I just wanted to
get on a plane and head to a far away place like New York.
"If anybody moves, I will burn him along with the whole
barrio", threatened the policeman who had shot the man,
pointing his gun at  people standing there. I was standing
behind an electric pole, crying, my heart shattering into
pieces. I was overwhelmed with such fury that I wished I
had a real gun to shoot the aggressor. Suddenly, I saw the
old man revive and get to his knees, but now he had his
knife in his right hand. The policeman walked up  and commanded him: "Drop the knife." The old man, in excruciat-
ing pain, replied: "I have not violated any laws. I prefer to
die like a man." What happened after this marked my life
for a long time. Cold bloodedly, the police officer shot the
man a second time: "Bang!" This is how a deep rejection
towards police authorities began to be birthed in my life.

# 3
# SKYSCRAPERS

What a difference between New York City and San Pedro de Macoris! Although San Pedro is a very famous city, anything in Macoris that carried a New York stamp was considered better than anything "criollo," indigenous to the island. However, now that we were actually living there, I felt like I was being deprived of my freedom. Sadness overwhelmed me. I missed the freedom that I had felt in my hometown. In New York, the parks were very clean and structured; all the streets were paved, different from the dusty ones of Macoris. Skyscrapers, like the 87–storey Chrysler and the 102-storey Empire State were amazing. Yet I fantasized about going back to the old house made of wood and palms. How I needed my friends, my brothers and my cousins! I felt so alone.

My mother had bought me a brand new bicycle. But I would rather have had the wood scooter with iron wheels that I made with my own hands. To ride my bike, I needed an adult along to supervise. Back home, on my scooter, I could just run in the road with my friends. Although my mother and stepfather loved me very much, I felt bored at home, like a bird in a cage!

## Kept away from church

One Sunday, my uncle, Pastor Antonio Jimenez, took me to church. As we came into the sanctuary there were some men praying out loud, kneeling in front of the altar.

One of them stood up and walked up to me, hugged me, and took me to the altar. When he began to pray over me, others surrounded me and laid their hands on my head, shoulders, back, and even on my feet. They were all praying out loud. One of them raised his voice over the others and, weeping said: "This child belongs to God! Brothers, this child belongs to God. This child has a great calling from the Lord upon him!"

I returned home and found that a number of mother's family friends were visiting. They were playing bingo, dancing, drinking beer and liquor, and smoking so much that my eyes were irritated just from stepping into the small apartment. My stepfather, Delfin, was drunk. He met me at the door and stared at me.

"You better watch out not to let your Uncle Pastor brainwash you." Mocking him, he continued, "That guy laid with so many women and drank so much alcohol-- now he wants the whole world to convert".

The following Sunday, when my uncle came for me to go to church, I wasn't home; my mother and stepfather said it was better for me to go to the movies. To them, the movies were less harmful than church. When my mother told my uncle that I was at the movies, he was deeply disturbed and, pointing at her with his right index finger, said: "You have made the mistake of your life. You will cry tears of blood for Salvador for many days. Juanita, that child belongs to the Lord!" When I came back from the movies, my stepfather commented on the incident and mocked my uncle as the 'Hallelujah' hypocrite.

# Baseball in New York

As the days went by I adjusted to my new lifestyle. I made many friends in school and on the baseball fields. Baseball was my favorite sport. Since I had begun playing ball in Macoris, I made lots of friends. When someone got first choice in picking players for a team, they picked me. I began playing like most of the kids in my town: batting rocks or balls made from rags and catching them with gloves made out of cardboard or a thick tarpaulin. During my first organized baseball game, I hit two home runs, batting the ball out of the park and into the adjacent stadium, Tetelo Vargas, where professional baseball is played in San Pedro de Macoris. My dream was to play in the major leagues and become a professional baseball player like Roberto Clemente, Willie Mays, Mickey Mantle or Rico Carty who became the hero of everyone in Macoris.

Anyone who knew me, knew I had dreams of turning my abilities into a bright future. But then reality hit. I began playing in a league that met in New York's Central Park. Despite the fact that I had a new glove, none of the captains chose me. Finally, when one of the rosters came up short, they called me over. "'Chiquitin'(Shorty), come here and play right field." But after the first game I had no problems getting to play second base, third base or short stop, which were my regular positions.

One day, as we were practicing for the all-star game, I smelled something burning. So I asked my friend Furia: "Why is it that this place always smells like something is burning?" "They're smoking weed," he said. I had seen many grown men smoking, but since this had to do with my teammates, I decided to check it out. I approached the group and could see they were enjoying themselves. Though their eyes were very small and bloodshot, they were laughing hilariously: "Don't hog the joint, pass it on", one said. "Great high, man" said another.. "This is great weed !" they would say to each other.

During the second year of baseball season that I played at Central Park, the opposing team left their bag with bats, gloves and balls. A teammate that had a reputation for being a thief said: "If we take the bag we'll have lots of gloves, balls, and bats." I saw his suggestion as an adventure, and to show him and the rest of the team that I, too, was bad, I went along with his idea. We took the bag and divided the spoils on 108th Street and Columbus Ave., which at that time was the den of juvenile thieves.

Another day my friend Rony and I were in the same neighborhood when an interstate bus stopped at a light. "Whoever dares to take one thing off the bus' storage is the bravest." Rony challenged. We both ran off at full speed. I got there first, opened the storage door and took a bag. "A thief, a thief", yelled the people inside the bus. When the driver managed to get off the bus to see what had happened, it was too late. Rony and I were turning the corner of 108th and Columbus Ave. Later we sold a camera that was in the bag and in exchange bought a bag of marijuana for five dollars.

## Under surveillance

My misdeeds were noticed as the days went by. One of my mother's friends caught me red handed several times. I thought that the snooping old woman had to be a witch. She seemed to be everywhere. I would even see her in my soup. When I began smoking cigarettes, she was the one who discovered me. If I ditched school to meet with a girl friend, that day she would show up at my house with some excuse and if I was off-guard she would check my room to see who was with me. Whenever I had a fight with someone in the neighborhood, she was there. Finally, my mother asked very concerned: "Son, my friend Agripina is saying to me that you and Rony smoke weed. If you continue like this I will have to send you off to the island for your father to fix you."

Agripina was getting on my nerves. When my family

was home after work hours or during the holidays, she would show up. My whole family — my stepfather and his daughter, Miriam; Margot, my aunt; grandmother Tata; my mother and even visitors to our home — were mesmerized by Agripina Once she had everyone's attention, she would begin speaking about the lost condition of young people. After speaking generally about drugs, premarital sex and violence, she would close her statements saying: "I'm not saying this because of Salvador, but because of the youth of our days.They are not as we were. In our time, there was respect."

I denied everything Agripina said. And despite my mother's threats of sending me to the Dominican Republic, to my father's house, I kept right on doing what I wanted. I became a professional hypocrite. I certainly did not want to leave the great City of New York. The one who had cried to return to San Pedro de Macoris, was now bending over backwards to stay.

## Fun wasn't always fun

Rony and I got into dancing. Each weekend we were at a discotheque or some sort of party. To stay in fashion, "tirando tela" as we would say, we learned to pressure our parents and if they didn't give us what we wanted, we would go into the stores and just steal our favorite clothes.

"There's a big party going on in the Bronx — whispered Rony straight into my ear, as we rode the subway. "we're gonna' have fun."

We headed for the "fun" but once we got inside, we felt strange. As we sat in the luxurious room with dimmed lights, a male dancer came out half naked. "It seems homosexual," I thought, while taking another drink and puffing a joint.

"These people are totally from the other side," whispered Jovany, the youngest of the three of us. "I think we've fallen into a trap" After a while of drinking fine wine and smoking marijuana came the blunt invitations.

"Come into the other room with me, Negro,"invited one who'd been talking to me during the party;. A bitter taste welled up in my mouth as if I'd just taken poison. I rejected him. He invited me again, with the same result.

He attacked again. "You aren't into anything, Moreno?"

"Open the door, I'm leaving,"I said, quickly grabbing a great quantity of drugs from the glass table. I put them in my pocket defiantly. I made him believe I was taking a knife out. Suddenly, all of my friends came out of the rooms they were in.

"What's going on here?"

"Let's take off right now!"I said, taking advantage of the half-open door.

My family was very concerned about my attitude. On one occasion, grandmother Tata "consulted the cards" and said: "You have some very bad friends; if you continue like this, you will have me die of a heart attack."

My mother desperately wanted to see a change in my life so she moved frequently. She decided to move to Boston, Massachusetts, where the other part of the Jimenez family lived. Naturally, I had to leave against my will. Our move was immediate, as if we were fleeing from someone.

## No sanctuary

In Boston, Aunt Luisa helped us find a beautiful apartment. Since we knew no one besides Aunt Luisa, we spend most of the time at her house. The few Hispanics that lived in the Dorchester sector and those who visited from New York would meet there. Almost every weekend and on holidays there was a fiery argument or fight at Aunt Luisa' house because of the amount of drinking. The house of harmony would turn into a tavern of discord. One time, after everybody had said goodbye, Luisa called to us, yelling at Chino, my cousin and I: "Run, he is going to kill me". Rito was there, laughing as he jabbed at her boxer-style, mocking and making faces.

"Come on, Luisa, punch my face," he said, moving from side to side, jabbing at her. When we tried to separate them, Rito punched us too. He made a grave mistake. Chino and I beat him up. We broke every glass item in the apartment. Not one piece of furniture remained in its place.

"Give it to him! That abuser! Give it to him, good! " Luisa egged us on.

The next day, Rito showed up at our house in Roxbury to excuse himself, even though he had taken a beating that left him with a bumpy face, black eyes and scratches all over his body. He was a good man. Chino and I got along with him, better than any other person, but drunkenness had transformed him.

At the new school I began to have problems from the first day. The fact that I came from New York and dressed like a New Yorker caused jealousy in local gang members. They started putting me down and challenging me. About two or three months after I'd transferred, I had a problem with the gang leader and I chose to act. At that time, I knew a man from New York, called Pedro Colon. He was well known for being tough. He had gotten into a gunfight with the police on 108th and Columbus. Other criminals from New York that visited Boston respected him. Pedro was thin, weighed about a hundred thirty two pounds, and five

feet six inches high. Once, when a local hoodlum was trying to come on to my sister, Miriam, Pedro had taken care
of things. "I knocked him down so he doesn't disrespect you
again in front of people" he said, minutes after laying out
the offender with one punch. And even though Pedro was
thirty-two, twice my age, he treated me with respect and
taught me a lot about the streets. So I confided to him that
the following day a gang would be waiting for me at school.
He decided to come along. As I approached a group of students preparing to start the school day, I saw the man I was
looking for.

Without hesitating, I took out my knife. Everybody
started running, some were yelling, but two or three members of the gang had been waiting for that moment, and
broke out knives as well. As soon as we started stabbing
each other, Pedro showed up, balancing an iron pipe with
his hand. In the midst of the yelling and the confusion,
Pedro yelled: "Let's go, before la "jara" comes (the police).
Sure enough, the police passed by as soon as we ran out of
the school.

Pedro advised me that we should return immediately to
New York or we could end up in prison. I called my mom
as soon as I arrived in the big city. She begged me, for the
love I had for her, to go stay at Agripina's house. I agreed. I
didn't want to increase her pain. Weeks later, she decided to
return to New York.

After prevailing over the delay tactics of the  school
system bureaucracy, I was once again admitted to Brandeis
High School. Although they never discovered the Boston
school incident, I was soon enough involved in other similar encounters. Using martial arts fighting sticks or a golf
club, or a 007 switchblade became an everyday thing for my
friends and me.

"Never turn your back on anyone," Pedro would advise. "Sit with your back facing the wall and your eyes alert so that no one can take you by surprise. Hit first.Whoever hits first, wins the fight."

However, Pedro Colon, after a robbery, trusted a friend. Covetousness perverted the loyalty of this man towards his boss, and Pedro died, struck by several treacherous shots in the back. "That will not happen to me. I will die fighting, facing forward," I thought in my more reflective moments.

## Expelled from music

My friend John, who had graduated the same year that I did from Booker T. Washington Jr. High School, was now attending high school at Louis D. Brandeis. "I've got a lot of the blonde that put King Kong to sleep," he boasted, promoting the marijuana he sold. The following day, he invited me to meet with him and other students that had also graduated from middle school with us.

That morning we met in Central Park, just north of 80th Street, a few blocks away from school. Between the trees, on a rock, we began to smoke until the panorama began changing before me. Suddenly, the morning sun became very bright, the sky was bluer than ever, the trees were greener that ever. Conclusion: The park was paradise! I broke out in uncontrollable laughter. I felt as if someone were tickling my stomach, provoking me to irresistible laughter. Possessed by that laughter, I made fun of chubby Nordic: "Hey, you look like King Kong. Watch out, Tarzan of the monkeys is coming… ha,ha,ha!" Although he was 5 feet 9 inches tall, almost 2 inches taller than I, the effects of the drug made me feel bigger and stronger than him and my two other friends. We left and headed toward school, making fun of everything that came near us.

Finally, when I got to my class, I laughed at the paint-brush mustache, the bottle-bottom eyeglasses, and the Charles Chaplin suit my teacher wore. There was fear in his expression. He didn't know what to do: he barely was able to finish his class, trying to ignore my interruptions and tasteless jokes. The same thing did not happen during my second class. The music teacher looked straight into my eyes and scolded me. "Mr. Sabino, if you continue like this, you will not end up well. You'll turn out very bad."

I tried to cover up by playing my trumpet, but the teacher was not finished yet: "Those bloodshot eyes and clownish laughter have a lot to say for you. If you continue like this, prison is inevitable." Then I replied: "Look old man, I don't care about your sermons, I'm a man and I do as I please." I got up from my chair and approached him, as he was preparing to lead the band, and I threatened him: "I can bend this trumpet on your bald head, if you keep cursing me."

At that point the security guards came in and forcefully took me out of the music hall. They took me to the office of the principal, who was already irritated with me, and suspended me for several weeks and expelled me from the music department.

I felt my life was changing. Since very young I had learned never to raise my voice to an elder. I'd been taught to "respect gray hair". However, I was violating that principle outside as well as inside of my home. Some people that considered me an honorable person at one time, approached me in love and counseled me. Teachers, friends and family members would call me, take me aside, have me sit down to talk, but I just wouldn't listen. The only moment of peace that I had was when I visited the furniture store where my friend Modesto Cruz worked. I would spend hours every evening studying music and dreaming. "Do you really want to play the trumpet?" he would ask. "To be good at it you will have to sacrifice everything, or you'll just be one more in the crowd."

I devoted more time to music. A baseball season went by and I didn't play for the school's team or with Liga Juan Conde, the team I was supposed to play in that year at Central Park.

# Missing my dream

My great passion had been to become a baseball player for the major leagues, something that now was practically impossible. This sport was still in my heart. But, my baseball buddies went on without me — those with real athletic talent signed to play professionally. I never got to the majors. Besides that, my lifestyle was now adjusting to my new goal.

Smoking cigarettes, using drugs, drinking alcohol and dancing all night were harmful practices for baseball players. However, for a trumpet player such as I, this was very normal. Leopoldo, whom we called Furia, Ivan Jordan and Frank Spies, among others that played baseball with me, were very different from my new nightclub and discotheque friends.

One time, they sought me out and asked me to play with their new team: "Salva (as they called me), the team is good, but we lost the first four games because we're lacking a good second and third base player that is not afraid of the ball. We also need a power hitter.. We need you!" With all the flattery and my desire to play I just couldn't say no. But, on practice day, I was disappointed. Out of ten pitches, I think I only caught one or two balls, and those catches were shaky. I did better at batting but I didn't impress the new coach. On top of that, when the time came to run, my friend Leonardo Sisa, who had played baseball in San Pedro de Macoris and was now training another team, was standing by watching Because I didn't slide into second base, he yelled: "That's what lazy players do. Next time I want to see you eat dust."

Still, from the moment I began playing again, I felt much better. I began to get together with my old baseball friends. Generally, because it was summer, we would get together in front of a building that was near everyone and we would talk about the past games and baseball in general. If we were invited to a party, we wouldn't drink more than a beer and we would return home early to feel fresh the following morning to play in the next game.

Our team "Estrellas Dominicanas" was probably the city's first "dominicanyork" team. (This is what they call the Dominicans that live in New York) In spite of the team's name, not all of its players were Dominicans — there were players from other nations, as well.

When we reached the finals, the tension increased. We were very excited. During the third game of that series, I hit a triple. Furia, the captain of the team, who was next up to bat, gave me a sign indicating that we would do a "squeeze play", which meant bunting so that I could run from third base to home and score. What a surprise we got! The other team figured out our strategy. The pitcher threw the ball outside the strike zone and I was trapped, halfway between the bases. The catcher caught the ball and threw it to third. I quickly turned around while the ball was passing over my head. Running as fast as I could toward home, just a few steps away from my goal, I dove into the plate, tackling the catcher to the ground. The last thing I heard was "we love you' along with the voice of the fans. Then a player from the other team hit me in the back with a bat. As soon as I got my bearings and was able to see what was going on, I was afraid. Both teams got into a massive fight. A classmate called Pepe el Boricua ran after several people, beating them with some sort of oriental whip. Every time he lashed out, someone would scream and bleed.

Fighting off attacks with bats, stones or any object he could find, the opposing team's coach was bathed in blood. One of our teammates had hit him in the forehead with a bat. At one time, he had been my trainer; he was a good man who spent time trying to help the youth, not asking for anything in exchange. His only motivation was to bring hope to their lives. Some of my teammates and I came around him and stopped anyone else from disrespecting him.

Four members of a famous gang, who had been looking for trouble before that occasion, began challenging the players of our team. Suddenly, gunshots rang out. It was Mory and the Hippie, two youths from our neighborhood who had begun their criminal career. As always, the gunshots created confusion. People were running in every direction. While I ran toward the West of Central Park, I could hear people say: "The police are coming."

The next time we went to park, they broke the news to us that the league directors and the A division had suspended us indefinitely and had declared the other team as the 1975 champions.

I grew up at baseball parks. I grew up with a baseball bat in my hand; I loved that sport more than food. I played it in patios and alleys, with cloth balls, gloves made out of cardboard, and with bats made out of any stick I could get my hands on. Since childhood, my dream had always been to become a major league player. And even though in New York, I had had every opportunity to play: gloves, bats, uniforms, etc... every year that went by, my disillusionment was greater, and with that sad goodbye, my dream was dying.

Four members of a famous gang, who had been looking for trouble before that occasion, began challenging the players of our team. Suddenly, gunshots rang out. It was Mory and the Hippie, two youths from our neighborhood who had begun their criminal career. As always, the gunshots created confusion. People were running in every direction. While I ran toward the West of Central Park, I could hear people say: "The police are coming."

The next time we went to park, they broke the news to us that the league directors and the A division had suspended us indefinitely and had declared the other team as the 1975 champions.

I grew up at baseball parks. I grew up with a baseball bat in my hand; I loved that sport more than food. I played it in patios and alleys, with cloth balls, gloves made out of cardboard, and with bats made out of any stick I could get my hands on. Since childhood, my dream had always been to become a major league player. And even though in New York, I had had every opportunity to play: gloves, bats, uniforms, etc... every year that went by, my disillusionment was greater, and with that sad goodbye, my dream was dying.

# 4
# CHANGES

I committed myself wholeheartedly to the study of music. After graduating from high school, I decided not to attend the university because I didn't want to pursue an academic life, but one in the artistic field. My mother tried to persuade me in every possible way. My father called me from the Dominican Republic. Many of my friends also tried to convince me, but each effort was in vain. Finally, my mother said that if I did not attend a university, then I would have to find a job. Someone told me about a factory that was employing people to distribute neckties to stores and companies. Several weeks later they sent me to make a delivery. While en route I came across a friend and we began to smoke marijuana. I lost track of time and, when I returned to the factory two hours behind schedule, they fired me.

At a second factory, I was angry with the boss because he looked down on immigrants. There was also a worker who knew there were illegal aliens working there, and he would make fun of them when everyone was quiet by yelling "Immigration!" When he yelled that word, it made every single illegal run off and hide to avoid being captured and sent to back to their country. After a few days working there, while the boss was giving out orders in a tone of disdain, I grabbed my trumpet and walked to the door, when I heard him yell: "Where are you going?" I left the place without looking back. I worked because I had to, but what I really desired were the moments I had to practice with my

trumpet. As soon as my family moved into the neighborhood of 137th St and Broadway, we formed a youth band
called "Los Intocables"(The Untouchables). We practiced
any day of the week and at any hour. We had lots of enthusiasm; we were really like a family. We lived in mainly hung
around the neighborhood of Washington Heights. We partied in its streets. And soon they came to know us and love
us so much, that the people from the area and even well
known musicians were talking about our talent. We got to
the point were we alternated with El Gran Combo, Wilfrido
Vargas y los Beduinos, Hector Lavoe, Pete el Conde
Rodriguez, Chino y su Conjunto Melao, and other top Latin
bands. When we began our first recording, everything
began to change. Most of us not only smoked marijuana and
got drunk, we got high on cocaine, heroin and all kinds of
pills. Most of the well-known prominent salsa bands got
drunk with us; others with more experience advised us that
if we continued consuming drugs, our careers as musicians
would be failure.

The day I turned twenty I set myself a goal to do twenty marijuana cigarettes, one for each year of my life. The
result was that Manny, our drum playerpercussionist, and
others in the band had to take me out from behind a building and carry me home. The same thing happened with
other guys that played in the band. Some of us were arrested for drugs and several for alcohol abuse. But others were
wiser, following the advice of the mature musicians.

At the same time I played with "Los Intocables", I
began working with Ruben in a strap factory. One day that
I skipped work, a man driving a brand new Lincoln
Continental, said to Ruben: "would you like to make five
hundred dollars a week?" The following Saturday, Ruben
and I got together with the soviet Jarl Cocovic along with
his associate Pablo Perez. In a presentation of the company
"Futuristic Foods", we were challenged to make an invest-

ment of fifteen thousand dollars and we were guaranteed that in less than a year we would be as rich as the other franchise owners. We convinced our parents to lend us one thousand five hundred dollars each and form a company together, as owners of a fifth part of a franchise. Following this, we were presented with a plan in which we were trained to sell franchises.

Franchise salespeople owned cars and big houses, their commissions were over one hundred thousand dollars a year. They fed our ambition to such a point that we began selling franchises before finishing our training.

Some months later, as I climbed the company ladder and began working directly under one of the more prominent executives, he informed me that very soon government agencies, the Better Business Bureau and the IRS, would file accusations against the founders and leaders of this company. I spoke with my friend Pablo Perez and I told him I was very frustrated because I learned that the company was fraudulent. On top of that, I always suspected it because the big leaders, the richest ones, would frequently ask me about the best cocaine. They would come out in their Lincoln Continentals, Cadillacs and Mercedes Benz' to negotiate and practice what was unlawful.

I thought that at age twenty it was too late to start over. So in my desperation, I went along with a plan to rob a paymaster who almost every Friday carried seventy five thousand dollars with him. However, on the day of the robbery he was only carrying five thousand dollars in the envelope we took from him, according to the police report given to the news media. Later I learned that most thievery is perfect and easy when it's still in the planning stages. According to the plan, all we had to do was go to Secaucus, New Jersey, "surprise him as soon as he got out of his vehicle and the money would be ours."

# On the verge of freedom

The plan failed, and of course because of this armed robbery I was at the Bordentown Correctional Facility prison in New Jersey. In my time of reflection, negative thoughts would invade my mind. My criminal background would limit many of the opportunities that society offers. I would have liked to go to a music university, but who would employ me with a criminal background? Who would trust in me? In addition, even if I did still have opportunities, I felt that time was running out on me quickly and there was nothing I could do about it. In primary school I learned that time is gold. And if this weren't enough, I remember the day I got out on bail from Hudson County Jail. I went to Tony's house, a musician friend of "Los Intocables". His mother approached me, looking me straight in the eye and said, with much distaste: "Youth, a divine treasure wasted."

Anyway, if I did get out of Bordentown prison with a criminal record, my life did not end there; I also learned that every negative situation brings with it a seed of success. Although I had just turned twenty-four, I would not give up, I had my entire life ahead of me, and apart from that, the victory does not belong to the swift, but to those who finish the race.

My time of release was near. I had counted each day, but now my countdown was different. The other prisoners that were close to me began to count along with me, when we got up they would say to me: "Sabino, fifty days and a wake up." The following morning: "forty-nine and a wake up," and so forth, until the day I woke up to leave. Finally, the awaited moment arrived. I was taken to a room I had never seen before, and I was handed a suit that my mother had brought. I took off my prison attire and dressed up as a "paisano." It was a long time since I had felt like that. On one hand, I was anxious because of the time it was taking the officers to finalize the procedures and get papers signed. I wanted to go. On the other hand, I had a knot in my throat. Because of the love I had for my prison friends, I wanted to stay. But, it's human nature to prefer freedom and I really wasn't given a choice. I had to leave.

When I passed through the exit door, I remembered what the more experienced prisoners had advised me: "When you leave here, if you look back, you'll come back. Don't dare look back." But I never was superstitious. Although the correctional officer had instructed me to walk straight to my friends' waiting vehicle, hearing the sound of the prisoners calling my name, , I had to stop, turn back and look. At a distance, between the iron bars, I was able to see the silhouette of some of the prisoners who had been with me for a whole year. They waved their hands saying good-bye, waving white handkerchiefs that they would stick out the bars that were now separating us. I thought that some day I would see some of them, but of others I would never know anything again. That's how street men's goodbyes are. They remained in prison. However, I was now free.

# 5
# STREETS

Free at last! What an exciting emotion! I was finally enjoying the prisoner's ultimate fantasy: the Streets! The New York skyline had never seemed as beautiful as it did to me that day. In fact, everything was precious: the streets, the people, even the Port Authority bus terminals were beautiful in spite of some drug addicts, drunkards and homeless people using the sidewalk as their beds. To me, everything looked sweet. When I left the parole office and arrived at my house on 139th Street, between Broadway and Riverside, in Manhattan, I saw that neighborhood as a little piece of my city paradise. Someone said, and rightly so, that beauty is in the eye of the beholder. The neighborhood I'd wanted to abandon so badly I had risked my whole future now seemed like a spring garden to the eyes of this newly liberated man.

It wasn't spring though. It was the dead of winter -- January 20th, 1981. That afternoon, my friends threw me a welcome-home party. "El Lento" gave me a nickel-plated gun, a 38 caliber special Smith & Wesson, and enough cocaine for everyone. Miche brought two liters of brandy, and the rest contributed what they believed would bring happiness to the occasion. At the end of that day, my mother arrived after a hard day's work. The celebration became very different. Almost all of my family came by the house that night. Most of the gifts were simple pieces of advice to keep out of all illegal activities. As different as these celebrations were, these were the two worlds I had in front of me. Unfortunately, the world offered me a street life that was more attractive to me than a family life.

# White collar criminals

Three days after being released from prison I got together with my friend Pablo Perez, who invited me to the new company "Gemstones", of which he was vice president. He told me that after he left Futuristic Foods, the company that we had worked for, he went into the sale of precious stones. For a few days, I visited the places in New York where most of the transactions for the costliest precious stones of the world are conducted. The hotel Via Brazil in Manhattan, lodges most of the salespeople and distributors. Very quickly I learned to appreciate rubies, emeralds and diamonds, among other precious stones. As soon as I began linking up with the precious stones salespeople, I began to notice that many of them were as corrupt or moreso than drug dealers. Some would tell of their adventures and how they deceived the natives, buying stones in Third World countries and scoffing at airport security to later sell them in a developed country, making huge amounts of fortunes in two or three transactions. Others would just mock, exaggerating how they bought a stone of high value at a ridiculous price, basing it on a false appraisal.

Even knowing their modus operandis, I fell many times into their deception. One time they invited me to an open-air restaurant in the financial district of New York. Danny, the Austrian, introduced me to his friend, Pete. This man had a commanding voice. He was a man in his fifties, about five feet nine, white, blonde and very fit. He looked like a retired professional wrestler. Along with other two men of his age, he devised an extraordinary plan in which I would make two thousand dollars and the exclusive right to distribute all the cocaine that was transported. I only had to make several deposits at a commercial bank cashier. It seemed good and I accepted the proposition. Everything was to be coordinated from the inside. A sum exceeding ninety thousand dollars was deposited.

The boss said that another person was to pick up the money in cash at the arranged international bank by a stipulated time. The transaction was a success. That money was to be used to bring a load of many kilos of cocaine using one of the small Antilles islands as a bridge. The money was obtained quickly but the last part of the plan failed. The boss, who had described the drug smuggling with such ease and who, by his cunning in the financial transaction, had won everyone else's trust, would not be seen in the coming years. He was caught by the narcotics department in that nation..Even though he was an American with lots of money and influence, he was not able to buy his freedom. Instead, he got several years in prison. The other people in the operation managed to escape in time because a clever and risky pilot eluded the authorities and flew them to another small island.

# The heroin connection:
# a desperate former diplomat.

I detested being among those men that differed greatly in age, social class and in opinion, but ambition kept me glued to them. And, though I could see that they were corrupt and that it brought them trouble, I could also see that they were very smart and, very often, got what they wanted.

Danny, the Austrian, had been a very prosperous businessman and had a good reputation in his country. He became one of the most prominent ambassadors of his country; however, he was caught in a shameful iniquity of international proportions. He was judged, sentenced, deported and most of his possessions were confiscated. In

his desperation to get back to the top,, he focused on transporting products illegally from other nations into the United
States. Because of his influence, he was able to build a
smugglers' network for diamonds, emeralds and other precious stones.

Now he was the figurehead president for Gemstones, a
lawful company that supplied almost every type of precious
stone to the most luxurious jewelry stores of the "Diamond
District", in New York.

A few days after I began working as a bodyguard for
Gemstones, my friend Pablo Perez said that Danny was
very pleased with me, and that he wanted to invite me to
lunch because he had a proposition to make.

That day, Danny invited me into his office and began
asking me about my prison and street experiences. After a
long time of conversation, in the midst of laughter, he said:
"You are the man I've been waiting for. Listen to me. I want
to confide something to you that can possibly make you rich
in less than a year if things work out right. You're not a man
that can live a long time depending on a salary, as good as it
may be," he said in a tone of wisdom or like an actor who
knows his script very well.

Danny was not very tall, but his knowledge, influence
and experience were what undoubtedly made him a big
man. He left me alone for a few minutes. Then he returned
with a package in hand and said: "Sal, when I passed
through Bangkok, I met a friend who told me that here in
New York, this article is more valuable than diamonds."
While he was talking, he opened the package.

Instantly I knew what it was about. Danny had a package in his hand that contained the most coveted dust of the
big cities: Heroin! "They tell me there are different qualities
of this drug. Why don't you take it with you and try it out?"

By this point in our conversation, I had already figured
out that someone with very little experience had given him
his information on the value of pure heroin. "Please, take

this package. Try it,"he said. "Let me know if something can be done with this. I have about another kilo and I can get any quantity of it." he handed me the envelope that contained approximately thirty grams.

# Dealer's jackpot

I wasted no time. Danny didn't know what he had. And there was no doubt that this could be the biggest connection I would ever have. I had heard of cocaine kilos but never about kilos of pure heroin. As soon as I arrived to the neighborhood, I called Benny, who at that time had been released from the Bordentown prison. He spent all of his youth injecting himself with heroin. He was one of the few guys that would inject drugs anywhere in his body. Benny could easily get around any alarm system to plunder his victim. He used to do the difficult upscale jobs. One time he managed to break into a house of a high-ranking military leader and extracted more than one hundred fifty thousand dollars in valuables and cash. He placed a great part of his loot at my disposal: "Look what I have here for you my friend. This is for you. Do want to take it now o later. And take something to my 'madre negra'", said Benny with the affection of a good friend toward my mother.

I didn't pay much attention to what he said. I was too excited thinking about his probable reaction when he saw what I was about to show him. I took out the heroin package. He opened his eyes and said: "This is not cocaine. Compadre, all of this can't be for us alone, right? Don't joke with me! We're rich!" he exclaimed without letting me say one word. Next, we went to a place called "shooting alley", where drug addicts hang out to inject themselves.

What a horrible place! The young seemed old and the girls looked unresponsive. "Hey dude, try this out" asked Benny, to someone who resembled a rat and seemed to be the leader. "Chino, come here, put some of this into your stew, commanded the leader."

Several minutes passed. Chino diluted the heroin in the hot pot over the fire, and had   a friend help him find a vein in his thin arm with some sort of tourniquet.  Then Chino took the needle, extracted only one dose, and began to inject himself. Suddenly, he fell violently.

"Nobody move. Anyone that moves gets the bullet," I yelled with my gun in hand. "Friend, take it easy. This dude is suffering an overdose. Don't you understand?", yelled Benny.

"Give him two spoons of salt", somebody hollered.

When the young man appeared to be safe, someone who looked like he had been locked up in a basement for several days fixed his eyes on me with admiration. He appeared to be sixty years old, but I'm almost certain he was only about thirty something. "Do you have the one that put King Kong to sleep?" he said with his dry, withered lips and the few yellow teeth he had left, referring to the purity of the heroin. "Watch out. From now on, you'll have to walk the streets with eyes in the back of your head."

# 6

## SALES

### Assembling the team

The news broke out all over Washington Heights and its surrounding areas. Soon afterward, people with big connections started contacting us. Vitin "el Lento" had an apartment ready to distribute cocaine on a large scale, so that became headquarters. We hired some heroin experts for processing.

Those who were the closest to us would take care of security and transactions: Benny, Bugs Bunny, Ruben and Genito, whom we had recently brought from Puerto Rico. However, Old Man Lee would be in charge of drug preparation. . "I'll work day and night if I have to. This stuff is deadly. It will sell big time," boasted old Lee. Despite his cheery disposition, he was a cold blooded and meticulous assassin.

The old man won my trust the first day I met him due to the fact that he had been part of the Oscuro Nolin gang. They were one of the first to launch into drug dealing in Washington Heights. They were tough and loyal to each other. I had heard about how Nolin and Lee went out to avenge the death of a comrade who had been killed in the streets by a rival gang.

In the middle of a turf war, Nolin and Old Man Lee caught the other gang's members checking out their meeting spot, and planning to eliminate their competing cocaine operation. Old Man Lee and his companions shot two of their rivals right there in the middle of the street and followed a third to another state, where they killed him. I had heard this from a friend and in the street warfare chronicles that regularly made the rounds.

On the streets, the man who carries out vengeance always gains the respect of the rest. In fact, anyone who fails to avenge the death of a friend is marked as a coward. In street law, friends protect each other. Ironically, they also often end up turning on each other.

But Lee, had a record for standing up for his gang so, despite his being the newest member, I felt comfortable with his involvement.

When things were in order, we began to distribute.

# Living the lie of the drug life

Soon we made contact with distributors in the city, in several other states, and even in other countries. I knew a little about drug dealing because of my experience in nightclubs. I had also naturally picked up an awareness of the way things worked because of the neighborhood in which I lived all of my youth.

But now it was different. Like a student who'd been promoted, I could say that I graduated from the prison university. But now I needed to pass Street 101 by gaining some street savvy. Many young people don't study and they consider sacrifice something antiquated. If they only had an idea of the great price that must be paid on the streets, surely they would take a different road.

Danny the Austrian, arranged to meet with me at my friend Pablo Perez's house. There he received me along with another man also named Danny. This guy was an evangelical Christian. "Come in, God bless you. Danny left this for you", he said, delivering me a package with his left hand, and holding the Bible with his right hand. "Thank you", I answered, wondering whether he had any idea what was in the package..

I assumed he didn't. It turned out to be a load of heroin that had a value greater than four hundred thousand dollars. I'd been on the street for many years but had never seen anything like this before. A man with a Bible in one hand and tecata, as they call heroin, in the other; my friend Belly Joe cracked up over that as we drove from Queens to Manhattan.

# Good business and a guilty conscience

The apartment truly resembled a heroin lab. Preparing heroin involves diluting it from its pure state into a lesser quality, then getting it to bond with other chemical agents. All the top sales people would come to the apartment for supplies. In one of his last visits, Joe Black, who was one of the main distributors in Harlem, surprised me."Hey, Pana," he said, "I've done real good working with you. I've got my new Cadillac and everything I want. And look, this year we've been so lucky we had to blow away very few people".

"What do you mean you had to blow away...?" I asked.

"Don't you get it? In this business you have to shoot those who don't fulfill their duties so that people respect you?" Joe replied. "More people die in Harlem for the sake of this dust than for gold and diamonds," he said laughing, in imitation of a Hollywood movie hit man.

A chill entered my bones. I recalled the warning of a friend that had more street experience than I. He warned me that the sale of heroin would bring more blood than had the cocaine trade. He added, with emphasis, that heroin would bring a curse to Washington Heights: "That diabolical dust. Whoever doesn't die of a bullet, dies of an overdose," he would say, trying to persuade me to sell cocaine, which according to him, was less harmful.

Joe Black's report opened my eyes to the effects of drugs in the streets. I felt guilty. But I told myself I had to continue living and it wasn't easy to change my lifestyle.

# A sale to Tio Juan

One of our top cocaine connections in Washington Heights spoke to us about an intimate friend that had a "tio" (uncle) who bought heroin on a regular basis. He insisted that I do the transaction directly with him. Tio Juan was coming from outside the country the following day and had asked for an initial buy of about thirty grams of heroin. The afternoon of that same day, we met at Manhattan's Central Park.

"Sorry for my delay, Pana. Something happened at my warehouse", apologized the friend that had recommended Tio Juan and his two nephews.

"I came here because you insisted that I meet with uncle because he would be a client of caliber and that everything would go all right, but..."

Coolly, calmly and pleasantly, he interrupted me. "What's happening, Pana? A fighting cock like you is not going to get scared at this point in the game."

Five minutes later, the uncle and his two nephews

arrived. My friend handed the heroin to him. Following that, the uncle walked up to the car, and sat in the back seat where I was, without asking permission.

"How are you doing? You must be the man." He greeted me, then passed a roll of papers in front of me while touching my left shoulder in an effort, it seemed to me,, it seemed to me, to see my face.

"Stay still, old man," I warned, pointing at him with a 380 caliber pistol and blocking his vision with my left hand. "Get out of the car without looking back so you don't trip and fall,"I yelled, while Benny escorted him outside with his nickel-plated 357.

"Your violence staggers the imagination," my friend complained, as he took us quickly out of the neighborhood.

"That uncle guy smells like shrimp. That guy is a "federuco" (FBI agent). He smells more like a cop more than anybody in uniform. The nephews are a pair of cowardly informants who will soon pay the price for their deception," I replied bitterly.

"Somehow, loco, they've paid, doing time with me in Sing-Sing," he reproached.

But the following days proved that I was right. Since "the uncle" was not able to arrest us, for lack of information, he imprisoned others who fell into his sophisticated city-wide trap. He broke up another ring, whose members were imprisoned for fifteen years in federal prison.

# Keeping a low profile

I avoided unnecessary contacts. I spent time in seclusion. My friend the negotiator, who introduced me to the "uncle" people, sent a message from his hiding place saying that even though people didn't know much about me, I shouldn't check in at the office or leave any kind of trail because the slightest clue could lead to arrest. I took his advice and stayed away from work for a month.

In addition, at that time I was having problems with Danny, the person who supplied the merchandise. I owed him almost a hundred thousand dollars and the bill was due. He began sending his debt collectors and threatening me over the phone. Everything had been so easy, but now every man had learned to survive the streets on his own. Even that educated, sophisticated and extremely intelligent man had descended to the depths of the underworld and learned to behave accordingly. Finally, he personally called and threatened and warned me that if I didn't show up and pay his money, he would call my parole officer and have me arrested. He proposed a private meeting, and I accepted.

I met him at noon on the corner of Broadway and 207th Street in upper Manhattan. We were both on time.
"Did you bring the money?" was his salutation.

"Did you know that "chotas" (informants) are the most undesirable people in the streets? If you turn me in, you will always be considered a rat," I said, clenching my teeth and pointing my index finger at his face.

Just then, I saw some cars at a distance and suddenly three white men came out of them. Instantly, I knew they had to be "associates" from Bensonhurst, Brooklyn, as he had boasted.

I reacted quickly. "You broke your word, you stupid old traitor. Here, this is for being a chota." I insulted him and began to punch him all over until he fell near the trunk of a parked car.

Immediately, I fled, pushing the people that blocked my way. The screaming women and the possibility of being caught by the supposed associates made me run faster than Lou Brock stealing home. I reached Rony's house. I armed myself with a gun and convinced myself never again to go out alone or unarmed.

My life completely changed. I had violated the terms of my parole. And now I needed to protect myself from my enemies. To make it worse, I also owed them a great deal of money. I was no longer able to visit public places. Wherever I was, I suspected everyone I saw. I was afraid that either a police officer was getting ready to arrest me or a paid assassin was looking for the right moment to kill me.

*Two Ways*

# 7
# ADDICTIONS

After that I would rarely walk the neighborh o o d streets. Everything had changed. If I left the house, I would go straight to "the spot ", as we called the apartment from which we distributed the drugs. I traveled only in taxis. Since we were no longer working with Danny the Austrian, we began buying cocaine with the heroin profits. The day we sold what was left of the heroin, I came down with a bad cold, congestion and aches and pains in my back.

Riding in a taxi with a friend named Matt, I began to complain about having the flu. "What time did you take your last snort? " he asked, meaning when had I sniffed my last dose of heroin.

"I have never sniffed tecata," I answered.

"But you've been cutting the stuff?" he insisted

"Yes. What does one thing have to do with the other?" I replied

"If you cut pure tecata without wearing a mask, you're more addicted than anyone.

You're addicted to smack," he concluded in the tone of an experienced tecato(addict). "You don't have an ordinary monkey. You've got King Kong on your back," Matt laughed.

"You have the guts to call me an addict?" I challenged him.

"Look, I think Pastor has some smack. Let's go to his house. I'm sure he'll let you have a good sniff. If you take that stuff and the symptoms disappear, it's because you had the monkey on you," he said carefully, trying not to offend me further.

The greatest dishonor of that time was for a young man to be called an addict. I had tried almost every type of drug, starting when I was very young. I even tried heroin out of curiosity. But me, an addict?

I took Matt's proposed test and to my surprise, after inhaling the chocolate-laced powder, I felt such a relief that I had to admit, just to myself, with a deep sigh: "The truth is that I am an addict." Of course, I kept the secret as best I could.

But things took a turn for the worse when a new habit was introduced to the drug world. I learned about it when a woman who wanted an excessive amount of cocaine contacted me. By the way she talked, I could tell she was an experienced buyer of large quantities of perico, which is what we called cocaine. I took her by the apartment to try out what we had. The guys were working. She took out a glass pipe and a glass flask containing a little ammonia. She poured the powder in the flask and mixed it with the ammonia. In a few seconds, like magic right before our eyes, a rock formed.

Trembling, she put the rock over the mouth of the pipe. She lit the pipe and began to smoke. Then she began passing the pipe to everyone in the room. I can't describe what happened after that. I had heard how Richard Pryor, the comedian, spent his fortune in what was beginning to be called the rich man's habit. I now understood why. First of all, she needed more than one hundred dollars worth of cocaine to form the rock, and that was enough for only five of us to experience any type of sensation. We continued smoking all night. Benny was the first one to react. He started saying he was seeing policemen on the roof and throughout the building, conducting a raid. A quick check confirmed that the problem was ours. There was not a soul around during those hours of the morning.

After smoking for a long while, we concluded that we had experienced the most rapturous high of our lives. I inhaled my last dose and held the pipe up. We were all looking at it, enchanted, almost worshipful. "The day will come when people will kill one another to smoke a little rock in a pipe," I prophesied.

# Crack becomes master

I didn't grasp the depth of what I had just said. We felt too powerful to believe it anyway. So we continued drug dealing as usual. However, each weekend we would smoke crack, every night until daybreak. Then we began smoking it every day, at every chance, and every hour until finally we were totally consumed by it.

Not all of the guys were addicted at the same level I was. Some maintained a certain amount of control. "El Lento", my business partner, Ruben and Genito, among others, initially didn't get into it. Benny, who was one of the first to succumb, let down his own brother-in-law, and stopped visiting us. Benny and I got too used to it. Just as a fish bites on the hook and as a bird falls into the snare of the fowler, I fell into an addiction that deprived me of a sound mind. I lost all sense of shame. I began dragging myself through the streets of Washington Heights just like the serpent that was reduced to ugliness and condemned to crawl on its belly forever, eating dust as judgment and being cursed by the Almighty for deceiving mankind.

My friends would try to give me advice, but the drugs had taken control of me. Each day, I felt that I was digging my own grave. I knew I was being taken as a lamb to the slaughter and I felt incapable of offering any kind of resistance. I was in bondage to the desire for drugs.

Pablo Perez introduced me to a friend who was a big cocaine contact. He presented me with a challenge: if I sold the eighth he was going to furnish me with, he would supply all quantities I needed after that. But I wasn't able to do it. Addiction conquered. It had become a strong, enticing monster. As soon as I had those 125 or so grams in my hand, I went to Ruben's house. We smoked for a long time until hallucinations began. I ran outside the house with a .38caliber gun in my right hand, and the drug in the other. I ran from the corner of the United Palace Theater on 175th Street and Broadway to 192nd St. The police did not show up, and no one tried to stop me. To the contrary, they got out of my way as soon as they saw me running through the street at that hour of the night.

When I arrived at the drug den on Hillside Ave., I sat down and thought about how crazy I was. But then I continued my rampage. I took a taxi and got off on 135th Street to pick up Genito to come along with me for a walk in the neighborhood. As soon as we began smoking, I began to feel fear of my enemies. I thought that even Genito was part of a police plot to trap me. I took my gun out and kept a lookout all night waiting for the police or any of my supposed enemies.

## Fruitless efforts

An important connection had come from Colombia to New York, to get acquainted with me and to supply me with drugs. I arranged to meet with him at an apartment I had on 139th Street. As soon as we met, he informed me that a friend that now worked in Florida had referred me to him. I promised myself that I would not let this man down, and I didn't. During the following weeks we worked hard. The word went around that I had something directly from "the Holy Land," which is what we called Colombia.

One Friday night, we were celebrating a great victory. We were climbing like a rocket, with great speed. But we fell just as quickly.

"Why don't we do some crack? I've got a pipe," Ruben suggested.

"After this one, no more," I said in a commanding tone.

But we did just the opposite. We smoked until we had used up all of the drugs. When the connection arrived to collect, I gave him all the money I had and told him I no longer wished to continue working. He insisted that we continue. I got into debt again, and he said that if I was interested in paying him back, he had a way of helping me. There was a bar owner that owed him a great deal of money.

"You go into the bar, you threaten him, and you tell him that if he doesn't pay by the end of the week, you and your men know were his business is located. Tell him that the debt was given to you for collection," he instructed.

I arrived at the bar before sunset. By the description given to me by my connection, I was sure it was the right person. I approached him, opened up the guitar case I carried and took out a short rifle. "Nobody moves. Mister, — yes you — you have until next Sunday to deliver what you have promised. Someone will contact you on my behalf. In any case I know where you live. Don't make me come back here," I threatened.

In this way, I was able to pay that debt and many others, collecting at gunpoint and carrying out other vile deeds. Another connection sent me to rob a manager making bank deposits. Around noontime, the man was going to the bank on a bicycle. I saw the sack that, according to my instructions, held the money. The chauffeur was an expert driver, in spite of his young age. He suggested that it would be better to stage an accident.

"I'll nudge the bike and we take the money from him," he said. And that's what we did. What we didn't anticipate was common sense: an accident would draw the attention of the pedestrians on the main avenue in busy Queens County As soon as the cyclist fell to the ground, I came out of the car with a long-barreled Magnum 357. I threatened to shoot anyone who tried to interfere. I took the small sack of money and we left quickly.

I had done the job but it didn't end up paying the debt. I went to Benny's house, where we bought cocaine until we had smoked my entire share — three thousand dollars. Benny, for his part, had stolen jewels, which the next day we sold to a jeweler friend for a total of three thousand five hundred dollars. That didn't last long either. In addition to crack, Benny began injecting heroin. We fought over this. We separated for some days. The rest of the guys from our group told me that Benny and I were too addicted, and they feared we would die at the hands of our enemies, because we were too careless. I tried to stop smoking, but I couldn't. I was trapped. My addiction was shaking me like a leaf tossed on the wind.

# The addicts' den

I would now do anything for crack. My morale was so low that I didn't care whether I ended up in prison, the hospital or the cemetery. I became a common street hustler. I would stand on 163rd Street in Washington Heights, waiting for customers — even people I didn't know — to buy any amount. I would steer them to different drug dens just to get a dose of crack for myself. Every time I could get a quantity of cocaine I would come back like a rat to its hole, to Joe Blow's den.

People were drawn to Joe Blow. He knew how to treat everyone nicely. And he would share his drugs with those in need. I liked his attitude. I, too, liked to share with others, especially with those who were abused, those who'd been low in the world. Like me, they had lost everything. Many precious girls came and sold their virtue for a bag of dope or for a couple of doses of crack. I wouldn't allow anyone to abuse them in front of me. I got into a lot of fights for that.

In the drug den many strange things happened. When crack was smoked, you couldn't drop your guard. We'd use up the crack quickly, then become frustrated that it was gone. We would fight over the least little thing, only to hug each other affectionately once we were high again.

I was in a downward spiral. One day, a friend accused me of using my influence to take away an important client. As I was headed to my favorite drug den, I heard the manager shouting vicious insults at me from his car. We came face to face. We punched each other, while others got into the mix. A few minutes into the fight someone intervened, and I believe we were both thankful for the interruption. We were exhausted. We didn't have the endurance it takes. All of a sudden, we began mocking each other.

"You're old, Sal, it's not the same, la pipa and la tecata have you crazy," Marinito said, pointing at me as he doubled over in hilarious laughter.

"And you smoke so much, you look like a pipe," I laughed. "You know what, you're the most tecato of all."

After a while we went into the drug den and shared the pipe one with another. This young man did what I did. I was a role model to him.

Our families knew each other. And his end was heartbreaking. Someone who had fought with another man named Billy the Watchman, mistook Marinito for Billy and shot him several times. He ended up in a wheelchair and, a short time later, died.

On another occasion, some of us were free basing — smoking processed cocaine — in a small circle, as we usually did, and I heard someone yell an insult. I reacted by taking a 3- foot long piece of wood that was broken and pointed at one end and thrusting it into the neck of the person whom I thought was at fault. They took him to the emergency room very badly wounded. Those who were present began to notice that I was frequently not in my right mind. They warned me to stop free basing but every day I would continue putting myself in bondage to it. I spent day and night on 163rd Street looking for the next opportunity to free base. I was crazy!

# War with the other side

I returned from taking a client to a friend's drug lair. When I came back it was dark. The police were just about to conduct a raid. They were searching from car to car. They knew that the street vendors, unlike dealers who work out of apartments hid their stuff any place they could find nearby: building stairways, behind car tires, etc…

Boom Boom, one of the girls down the block, asked, "Are you going to let la jara (the police) take the packet lying there."

"Where?" I asked.

My friend Pepin promised he would shield me from any approaching police officers. Without hesitating, I took a packet from under a nearby car. Then I heard Johnny Chain and another person say that the package was theirs. It was too late. I was not one to give in easily, at least not when it came to my next dose of crack.

Pepin and I fled at full speed through the back of the

building. We knew the neighborhood very well. It would be hard for the police to catch us, if they even dared to follow us. Coming out onto 162nd St. and Broadway, we took a taxi to his house. As soon as we arrived, we smoked most of the twenty or more one–and-a-half-gram packages. He kept the gun that was inside the bag.

About two or three hours later, I returned to the neighborhood. 163rd Street was very quiet. I thought the police were still patrolling the area. Suddenly, a group of six men from the other side came at me.

"Where's the stuff?" asked the boss, Gold Tooth, who had recently killed a man for less than what I had done.

"What stuff are you talking about?" I yelled, pretending innocence.

"Shoot him!" he said, giving the order to execute me.

I spotted the glint of drawn revolvers. I summoned up the strength to work myself free from Gold Tooth , who had me by the arm. I jumped over the car. And to my salvation, someone was coming by on that same side of the sidewalk. I shoved him. I turned the corner at full speed and sensed that more than one man was coming after me. I ran about two or three blocks. I went in and out of several buildings until I lost sight of them. My heart was pounding. Then I sat on the stairway of a building I had entered. I couldn't handle myself. I was very tired. I fell asleep in that abandoned building and was awakened at daybreak by drops of rain falling on my face.

I reached home and slept until 2 p.m. The guys began to arrive. That same night, they told me, Pepin had a gunfight with the rival dealers. They also reported that Gold Tooth had mocked an old man, forcing him to leap and dance to avoid his gunshots.

At dusk, we went to 163rd Street fully armed. We entered two of the apartments belonging to the other dealers. Of course, only the workers were there. We ordered them to leave and not to come back to the neighborhood. In the third and last apartment, we found nobody so we broke the door down and took it over.

It seemed like the whole neighborhood was waiting for that moment. There was massive involvement. Abby el Cordobes and The Hyena, big distributors at that time, showed up with a big group of armed strong men. We quickly organized a guard at each building. Some of us, armed with long-range weapons, staked out the block from the roof. That night, the pipe was not lit. It was wartime. Heroin was allowed in a war, but crack, never. We turned off most of the street lights. The scene was set. In the early morning hours, Marino arrived. "The Commander makes his street entrance," said one of the sentries stationed at the corner building.

Many did not like him because he had killed several people in the neighborhood and constantly pressured others to sell drugs. He was a ruthless adversary, maybe the most feared in the history of Washington Heights. And he wanted to speak with me. I had to deal with him.

"Those people are dangerous. What are we going to do, man?" he asked me.

"We're at war — I insisted.

"I told you we have to get organized," he challenged. "Man, when are you going to quit the pipe?"

So we went to Old Lee's house to discuss strategy. Marino was very good at this because he had been a

Marine. Whatever he fixed his eye on was a sure target. After discussing a defense of our territory, and an offense in case the opposing dealers didn't come back, he had each one of the men who were with him commit to the cause. Before saying good-bye, Marino spoke about the gunman's destiny. He didn't know that his own death, at the hands of a police officer, was near.

"Whoever lives by the gun dies by the gun. I only want to die with my gun in my hand," he said. Everyone's eyes were fixed on him. After his bodyguards did their routine check, they announced that all was clear. We followed them, guns in hand, and behind us came the rear guard.

The drug dealers were very angry for some time. As violence increased, business decreased. Several young people were wounded during confrontations. Others were ambushed. Marino and his men fought off a well-planned surprise attack. He himself was wounded badly but survived to get his revenge, shooting two people.

Finally, negotiations led to a deal allowing the other drug dealers to set up in a different neighborhood. Everything settled down. We would see each other around the area, without animosity. I continued smoking crack and getting involved in other kinds of trouble. Some time later I ran into one of the participants of the turf war, at the city's Rikers Island prison. He told me he had wanted very much to shoot me but couldn't because his gun was jammed. Others also told me they had tried to shoot me but couldn't. "That guy has a saint protecting him," they would say.

# Wounded on 163rd Street

One night, Billy the Watchman and I were enjoying a smoke of our last "stew". We had assaulted a client who had bought a good quantity of cocaine. As a result, Billy got into a fist fight with a man who had been a boxing champion in the Caribbean, in his category. And even though Billy was taller, stronger and young, they spent several minutes without landing a punch.

"Come on, come on, give it to me right here," the old boxer taunted him, moving from one side to the other. Despite his agility, he took a couple of hits.

"Let's see you defend yourself now," Billy threatened. He went for the 357 Magnum that I had used in one of my recent assaults. He got near the old boxer and jumped on him in a rage. He tried to hit him on the head with the gun, but his foe was shrewd once again. Locked in combat, they both fell to the ground. I had just taken a smoke and I let go of the pipe. I jumped on them, trying to stop Billy from killing the man in the middle of the street. I managed to grab the gun by the barrel, and quickly tried to push him aside but the gun fired. I felt the upward thrust of the shot, but I continued trying to keep the situation under control. Seconds later, I saw that I was wounded. I began to bleed profusely. Kenny Kent and Moises, the bongo player from "Los Intocables," approached me.

"Sal, you've been shot. We need to take you to the hospital!"
"Somebody, call a taxi!"
I heard desperate yelling. Some of my friends picked me up, trying to carry me to Broadway to catch a taxi. I was in the worst pain of my life. Half conscious, I could hear people talking and screaming.

"He got shot twice. But the bullet didn't go through. Take care of him, Chango," I recognized the voice of the old Cuban boxer in the midst of crisis.

By the time we entered the medical center's emergency

room, and they put me on the stretcher, the pain was unbearable. My vision was blurry. But I was able to see the white shirt of a police sergeant's uniform. I could hear him speaking into my ear.

"Who did this to you? Who shot you?" he kept asking. He persisted and one of the young men who'd been out on the street cursed at him. I wasn't sure, but it seemed that he then got into a shoving match with the police during which I was almost knocked off my stretcher. Then I saw the white coats of the doctors who now surrounded me. They began injecting needles into different parts of my body. I felt one of them shaving the hair off my abdomen. "Maybe he'll live. He is young and strong. He could be too weak, though. I think he's an addict," said one of the doctors.

At that moment, I thought of my mother. I felt I was embarking on a journey to heaven. I felt close to my destiny, close to God.

"My God, forgive me. Take care of my mother," I prayed.

I woke up to see close around me my uncle, pastor Antonio Jimenez, my mother and other members of my family, including the girlfriend of my youth, whom I had neglected for drugs. After I found out that I was not an invalid but that the doctors had performed a colostomy I began to think that my addiction had gone far enough. "Enough!" I said, "I need to let go of this habit."

# 8

# CONNECTIONS

My friends often came to visit me at the medical center. Almost every one of them came by to visit. My active connections paraded before me proposing any quantity of drugs if I promised to quit doing crack myself. Among the visitors came the man to whom I practically transferred all of my clientele. "Mr. Dandy" was so thankful for the new business that he offered me work as his partner. After thinking it over, I accepted. I committed not to return to the habit. As soon as I left the hospital, I met with him and we began working.

I trained his workers to distribute aggressively. I formed a team to collect payments and to establish order and respect for the organization. We grew rapidly, because Mr. Dandy had a key connection. He was able to get a type of cocaine that was so pure it caused hallucinations very quickly. I called it "the deadly stuff." We soon became one of the fastest growing connections of our area. We had customers in every part of the city and bordering states.

## The deadly poison spreads

I had an idea of opening new spots to distribute both wholesale and in small quantities. We decided to do the wholesale at two strategic locations: one in the north and the other in the southern part of Washington Heights. In addition, we opened three spots for small quantities in the center of Washington Heights where most of the addicts and petty hustlers moved about. Our customers multiplied everywhere we opened the spots. The strategy produced a lot of money, and a lot of problems. As we grew, so did our wickedness and our enemies.

A friend from childhood, very close, informed me that a competing group had put a price on my head. So we took matters into our own hands and decided to attack before we could be attacked. Every morning I left the house ready for war. I wore a bulletproof vest and carried two or three firearms. Besides that, I wouldn't go anywhere alone. As it happens in this world, they threatened to kill my mother and the woman with whom I had lived for several months — Jessica — who was also armed. She feared no one. At least two bodyguards were with me at all times. If I had to go to a dangerous place, we would go in two cars with men and enough ammunition for any battle that might erupt. I delegated my responsibilities. And increased the use of heroin to calm my nerves.

Finally, I convinced my mother and stepfather to return to the Dominican Republic, as they had always dreamed of. Before leaving, my mother left me the Santeria figures my grandmother had taken with her everywhere she moved. Santeria is a popular religion, based in the Caribbean that tries to blend voodoo and counterfeit Catholic saints. The "saints" are counterparts to Christian saints, each of which can be called upon to intervene in the affairs of men. My grandmother had left her collection with my mother before returning to her country to die. Following the instructions of my mother and the witch doctor, I increased the number of "saints" on the altar to more than forty; I had both pictures and statues. I was dedicated to expanding the business. I no longer needed to be a liaison between connections, as in the past. We had become a top connection in our own right. The business continued expanding; however, without us realizing it, our downfall began.

# Violent collectors had no mercy

When we had sold a lot of stuff and it was time to get our money, we sent the collectors. These men collected in any way they had to: taking valuable belongings, kidnapping, torturing, etc... They would do anything to recover the investment. Many times they acted according to their own criteria just to maintain their credibility and salary, and not as they'd been ordered to do. To collect from Old Stick, they entered his apartment and moved all of his furniture into a rented truck. When he tried to stop them, one of the collectors, known as Coco Puffs, attacked him with a knife. My friend called for an emergency meeting to deal with this matter.

Another person was taken naked outside his hotel. In another case involving the son of a rich man, the father had to pay the debt to save his son. This caused us many troubles: he discovered that I was in charge and declared all out war on me. Because of this, I had to hide out for a while, not because I feared him, but because I feared prison. Because of that, I began to lose strength at several spots.

# Attacked from different flanks

I began visiting the spots from time to time. I would go around with a team of men, among them a man who had been a lieutenant in his country's army. I ordered them to do the routine check and they came back informing me, "All is clear." However, as I reached the third floor of the stairway in a building on 160th Street and Broadway, I heard police radios. I opened the hallway window and let fall a package that contained at least two hundred and fifty grams of cocaine and close to two thousand dollars in cash. I'd also placed two guns in it. I continued descending the stairway until I faced a police officer. Then came a second officer with a package in his hand. They asked me some questions and with a scornful smile walk away.

These two officers were well known for this type of acting. Of course, the guys preferred to lose material than to be arrested. We decided to keep that apartment inoperative.

We also had to close an apartment of small quantity sales on 163rd Street that on its first day had produced more than twenty thousand dollars. We called this spot "The Hustler's Den." Hustlers are street sales people who take customers to different spots, mainly to feed their own drug habits. The strategy of this spot was that any hustler that would bring in a customer, apart from getting a commission, would get the cure which is, cocaine to smoke or money for heroin before going to work. The customer would also receive a gift according to the purchased quantity and was guaranteed protection from any possible violence. This spot grew surprisingly every day. Almost every hustler was connected with us for the protection we offered. However, we had to close it because we employed a person who was wanted by the police. Apparently, someone turned him in.

Some days later, I was at home watching Eyewitness News on channel 7, when I saw how the six guys that worked at the spot on 166th Street and Audubon, were being handcuffed. They were busted and arrested. All of the evidence was on the table: a considerable amount of cocaine, a processing laboratory, according to them, a Thompson machine gun, a rifle and five to six guns. The news referred to this group at "La Mafia Dominicana".

The arrest was a hard hit to the organization. The police units dedicated to fight drug deals were very smart and managed to close many spots in a short time.

At this point many of the guys had become addicted and the need to use their preferred drug, made it increasingly difficult for them to remain faithful. On one occasion, I charged Ruben to protect another small quantity apartment on 163rd Street and he informed me that the drugs had disappeared. His explanation was that the rats ate all the cocaine. He suggested that before opening a spot we should call the exterminators. Years later, he confessed, humorously, that he'd been the only rat in the apartment.

## Addiction speeds up the downfall

The downfall of the organization was inevitable. By this point, I couldn't seem to concentrate on doing business. I stayed home, taking heroin and cocaine. Now I was smoking marijuana mixed with cocaine. We called it diablito style. In addition, just to get out of bed, Jessica and I needed Genito to go out and buy us cocaine. At the time, I was sniffing so much cocaine that I would fall asleep anywhere, any time.

Coming back home from one of the spots, I fell asleep in a taxi and when I got out of the taxi I forgot a package of cocaine and a couple of thousand dollars. I had to inactivate the distribution site for a time. While things cooled down, I left my friend Roque in charge along with "the Hawaiian," a girl who had once saved me from a serious arrest. She stowed my guns in her purse, posing as my girl friend and walking me casually by police who were looking for me.

## Hallucinations and the final downfall

During New Year's Eve of 1982, after spending some time with the guys, Jessica and I arrived at our home, totally warped. During those first hours of the day, I was smoking frantically. My family was home. I thought that my mother and step dad had planned to turn me over to the police. We lived on the first floor of a building on 139th Street between Broadway and Riverside. Suddenly, I heard someone approaching my window. I pointed with my .45 caliber Colt Commander towards the window.

"There's no one there, baby," Jessica said.

"Are you also going to betray me?" I accused her.

"You're just freaking out," she defended herself while trying to console me with her caresses. I pushed her aside.

My hallucinations were transcending the real world. I used a stethoscope to listen to sounds coming through the walls and the heating pipes.

"Quiet! I'm listening to something," I said.

I always went around with my gun loaded, although the trigger was on safety. Right then, I pulled back the safety pin. I heard someone rubbing a gun barrel near the window. I had no time to lose. It was my opponent or I. The challenge was life or death. Angrily, I fired seven bullets, one after the other. The explosion produced such screaming and confusion that I ran out of my room to the armoire, where I kept my other weapons. Suddenly, my mother grabbed hold of my hip, and my step dad grabbed my chest. My clothes were drenched in blood. It seemed as if I had been shot, but my step dad noticed that the blood was coming out of lesser wounds on my hands and abdomen.

"What's wrong, man? There is no one there. Are you crazy?" my step dad yelled, frightened. I hugged my mother like a child in danger. After drinking a glass of milk, I calmed down. Then, thinking that the police could arrive at any moment, I packed my weapons, the cocaine and the money in a sack that I used to carry congas. At that time my aunt Margo and her husband Victor arrived and took the load with them. I left with Jessica through a different door and stayed at a hotel to keep out of danger. There I began to smoke again. I fled the hotel because I thought that the manager had a plan to trap me. That night, I ran from two hotels in the space of just a few hours.

I found out later that two neighbors retuning from a Christmas celebration, escaped my shooting by God's miracle. After this, the neighbors began to stay away from me.

We visited an apartment where we had set up a temporary operation, because the permanent tenant planned to live in it again.

A new friend called Forty Seven, who saved me from being caught at the raid in Audubon, was the one who recommended this apartment to us. We left another friend we called Old Stick in charge of the place. That night I began to smoke, against the will of those who knew me well. When my stuff was running out, I asked Old Stick to give me some of the stuff he had for sale . I promised to return it the following day. While we smoked, things began to happen. Jessica began to say that another woman known as Sussy was trying to tell her she was pregnant by me. She began to threaten her. When we had almost smoked all of the stuff, I was sitting on a reclining chair.

"Guys, turn off the lights," I ordered. "We're surrounded by the police," I whispered as soon as the lights went off.

In the mean time, I took cover leaning my back against one of the apartment walls. Then I looked out the window, peekng through the curtains. I saw no one and felt nothing. But then Jessica approached me and whispered that there was a strange sound coming from the living room armoire. I asked her to remain on guard while I took care of the window. Through the window curtains, I saw two police officers placing themselves in an attack position. I thought they were watching us with night vision goggles. Old Man Lee approached me to tell me that he feared that the police had us. We remained in suspense for while. I demanded that everybody remain silent by persistently making signs to them.

All of a sudden a forceful sound was heard from the living room armoire. Without losing any time, Jessica fired at the armoire. I began shooting at the police. I shot someone trying to come in through the window. I watched how one fell after the other while I was shooting. An unbelievable confusion arose inside the apartment. I saw Jessica on the floor. I took the caliber .38 Smith & Wesson special that she had used to fire. I opened the armoire door, and a cat went running out.

I noticed that everyone was running out of the apartment through the front door and decided to take the emergency exit. As I hurried down the fire escape stairs, my hat fell off and I noticed my hands full of blood. I put my foot down on the last step and two dogs began to bark. I was able to jump from one side of the street to the other. It was a risky jump, but I preferred that to going to prison.

As soon as I came out onto 156th Street, I heard a voice and saw Jessica's hand waving me over to a taxi. The driver didn't have the slightest idea of what he was getting into. I began giving him crazy directions: to the right, to the left, etc…

"Where are you going?" he asked. Immediately, I thought he was an undercover police officer. I told him that if he asked another question his life would be in danger; so I told him to keep driving. After two hours or so, we were on 96th Street and Broadway; I had to admit that all this was happening due to the degrading effect of drugs. I realized I was having another hallucination. I paid the taxi driver very well , although I think that what he was more interested in just getting out of that taxi alive. Admitting my ridiculous behavior, I said: "I will never smoke crack again."

But it was too late. I was ensnared like a rat , who sees the cheese but not the trap. Some days later, I invited several friends to a crack party and we smoked the last half-kilo of cocaine I had. This time I had fallen into a worse addiction than the first.

# 9
# ROBBERIES

As my business began to fail, I had no alternative but to sell the few belongings I had: cars taken from debtors, firearms and other things of value. I even looted what I had once considered sacred ground.

It was my practice to put a hundred dollar bill on my homemade altar every day, in front of the portrait of Mitricili, a female saint that witch doctors had told me gave me charisma with women and granted me protection. I would also stash money and other valuables in different statues. When I had built up a certain amount of money on the altar, I would take it as an offering to one of the witch doctors.

Jessica and I would kneel before the altar and place written prayers in and around the pictures, statues and candles of all sizes. Sometimes in the midst of this, Jessica would suggest we go to church. My answer was that those types of saints — the ones in church — had done nothing for us.

One day, when I had no money for heroin, I went to my "saints." I was careful to reach for the roll of hundreds inside one of the statues with my left hand because I had been taught as a child that if you picked up a cursed object that way it couldn't hurt you. Another day, I even raided San Lazaro — a very important figure in Santeria. I kept at it until, eventually, all the offerings were gone.

"Things are so bad, I even wiped out the saints," I told a friend as we smoked.

Then I lost Jessica.

We were traveling to lower Manhattan to see a friend who had a jewelry store and decided to sell a very valuable diamond I had given her as a gift. Three youths who were also trying to sell valuables at the store began arguing with me because I criticized their conduct. As the argument escalated, I went for my gun. They fled the store. I thought they were going to call the police and since, at that time, I was reporting regularly to a parole office, the last thing I needed was a new arrest . I asked Jessica to take the gun. We fled in two different directions. I escaped in a taxi but, unfortunately, she was arrested. We tried every way we could think of to bail her out, but it wasn't possible because other outstanding charges turned up on her record.

# Digging my own hole

Every day that passed, I felt I was sinking another inch. From time to time, one of my friends, doing well in the drug dealing business, would come to visit and bring me a gift or invite me to get high with him. Other times I would visit people in debt to me and pressure them to pay.  I reached the low point of having to take my best clients to friends just to earn the commission.  But I couldn't get ahead. So I decided to work with the gun again. I looked for Felipe, Forty Seven, and Chilly Willie among others to do "some work".

We hunted our victims like cats chasing mice. I had crazy ideas. The other guys were as desperate as I was. What we had in common was blind addiction.

Once, when we ran out of drugs, we went to 163rd Street and found that all the spots had already closed. Clients were showing up but no one was there to sell to them. So I got the idea of taking over one of the active spots and pretending we were selling. So we did. As the customers arrived, we would take them to the apartment. Once they were inside, we would tie them up, to the heating pipe or other secure place. We did this for more than an hour., until the inside of the spot looked like a prison. We were beyond crazy. When the clients entered the apartment, we took all their belongings. Each client became a prisoner who needed to ask our permission even to speak. The last person to arrive was a wealthy man with his lover.

" I want something good. I want the best," he demanded. He was prepared to buy a large amount.

"At this place, we sell only the purest," said Forty Seven.

The moment he stepped into the building, I had my gun pointing at his face.

"Turn around and put your hands up," I ordered.
"Take everything but don't harm him," asked the woman.

He did not resist . He was carrying a lot of money. We decided it was time to go. In a couple of hours, we'd smoked away the spoils.

As soon as we calmed down, we planned our next assault .We knew we had to keep level heads or we would put ourselves in danger. We were put in touch with a group of men from another state. They were interested in selling a large quantity of electronics, televisions, sound systems, etc… When they said as a last resort that they would be willing to exchange the merchandise for pure cocaine instead of cash, we knew it was time to act. Of course, the amount they asked for wasn't at our disposal, but we figured out a way to work it out. We gave them a sample. They were impressed. We told them to bring the truck to our house. Our men helped them unload the merchandise, while their leader and I tweaked the other side of the transaction. After a while, the leader asked about the cocaine. I kept talking, saying that everything would be resolved shortly. The guys behaved very cordially, until the moment came.

"Nobody gets desperate. This is a hold up," said Chilly Willie, with a gun in his hand.

"Is this a joke?" exclaimed the totally surprised leader.

"Where did you steal all this stuff?" I asked sarcastically.

"Does that matter? " he objected.

"Ladrón que roba a ladrón tiene cien años de perdón," (A crook who steals from a crook has a hundred years of forgiveness) was my reply.

He sat back in his chair. He smiled. He couldn't believe what he was seeing. So he asked us to treat them decently, since they'd come from so far. And we did. We worked out a deal with some people in the neighborhood for the sale of the electronics. The guys made it happen so fast, I never even saw the actual equipment. The profits from the deal were smoked just as quickly. Some time after this incident the leader of the electronics ring met Forty Seven in a New York prison and he admitted that during the whole deal he never would have imagined falling into such a trap. With a sly smile he asked Forty Seven to greet me on his behalf.

# No thought of consequences

We never considered, even remotely, that we could be headed for prison, or even death. We didn't think about it nor did we care.

One time, received information about a transaction with a very powerful dealer., who was not from our area.

We were proud of our respect and loyalty to the dealers on our block. We even made efforts to protect them. Many times we were out to scare the "gatilleros" that came from outside or that just sprung up in our neighborhood. A Colmbian woman, who was a connection, was assaulted in Belly Joe's building. Within a couple of hours , we had pulled one man out of his hotel and another from his own house. We held them until eighty percent of the stuff was returned.

Now, once again, we were dealing with someone that did not belong in our neighborhood.

We arrived at the location for the deal only to learn that the connection was crossing the main avenue one block over. We quickly spread out. In a few seconds, I faced them and began walking towards them. There were a lot of people on both sides of the street. It was a very sunny summer day. It was a very risky operation. In addition, they knew how to work. The top man was in the middle with the "mule," the one who carried the load. The other three served as bodyguards. I could tell by the way they were positioned that they were very well armed. However, this would not intimidate us from claiming our prize. It was imperative that we give a surprise hit but it had to be a sure thing, even though our cold blood didn't allow us to consider this as a matter of life or death. Our adrenalin was kicking in, preparing us for another adventure. When I was about twelve feet away, I took out my Luger, a 9 mm automatic pistol. "Nobody move," I commanded firmly, trying to intimidate them.

I held the gun close to my waist so it wouldn't be seen from far away. I took short steps forward, glancing from side to side, to keep control of the situation.

Everything synchronized perfectly. At that same moment, Forty Seven got control of the mule's load, making sure not to block the line of fire. The rest of my guys took care of the leader and the bodyguards. Suddenly, one of the bodyguards ran off screaming for his life. A young boy from our group, who was called Picky Louis, had stabbed him with a bayonet. After disarming them, we ordered them to leave. We told them to walk normally without looking back. We ran, got into a car that was waiting for us, and fled.

That whole day and night, we hid in a motel with a group of girls from the neighborhood.

# Willing to die fighting

We got word that hired bullies were patrolling the neighborhood, searching for the perpetrators of the hit. They were offering good money for any information that would expose those responsible for the frivolous attack on their connection. I imagined that if they were truly offering a good amount of money, it wouldn't be long before they bought someone in the neighborhood. The old technique of posting a desirable reward never fails in the streets. There is always someone ready to sell out for money. In fact, it didn't take long before we found out they were directly inquiring about me.

So we went to the last place they had asked about me. We left a message that we would come back as soon as they sent for us. After this open challenge, we decided to be more ready than ever. We didn't abuse drugs for some days. We no longer visited public places. We were aware of the imminent dangers. I decided not to have women in the house. Neither did we want any women hanging out with us. And I would not allow any friends, except those included in this war, to come and visit me.

One day Abby el Cordobes and the Hyena who were in hiding just like me, because of violent acts, wanted to see me privately. I had deteriorated significantly because of my addiction. They were still active as dealers. A new day had dawned. After sharing a few precious moments, they walked me home. We entered my building. As soon as I opened the entrance door, we saw a man with a sack in his hand and a newspaper under his arm. We each aimed a gun at him.

"If you move, you die," said Abby el Cordobes.
"You seem to be tough, pal," the Hyena said mockingly.
"What's happening?" the man asked, extremely frightened
"Who sent you?," I asked.

While we checked his sack and the newspaper, a man we knew from the neighborhood came into the entryway. They also put him under the gun.

"What's happening, neighbor?" asked the man who had just arrived, looking at me.
They were going to their jobs in a factory. We confirmed that quickly. I had rarely seen that neighbor in the building before. But everything seemed to be in order; he had his lunch very well packed in the bag. We said goodbye cordially.

Lee "el loco", one of the "Hermanos Valientes," informed me that a connection from the block wanted to see me because he had gotten information that I was trying to muscle in on his business. I assured him that I was willing to meet with them because I didn't mess around with neighborhood people. While approaching his territory, I turned my gun over to him as a sign of good faith. As soon as we entered the apartment, one of his men went into attack mode, going into a boxer's stance. But I didn't let him to intimidate me. Lee and another man there asked him to calm down. They had a table with several chairs in the room. Slim asked me to sit down.

"Why are you trying to intimidate my workers while I'm gone?" asked Slim with the cool posturing neighborhood guys used when they wanted to intimidate someone.

"What are you talking about? When did this happen?" I asked.

"Cuff him," someone shouted from the back.

I did not resist because I imagined a gun was pointed straight at my head. They asked me several questions. I responded with assurance because I was totally blameless and could prove it.

"You know very well that I have moved in on many other people. But if someone here can point out one single connection or one person from the block that I have taken something from, let that person shoot the first bullet."

It was true, so they let me go. They told me I was ruining the neighborhood, which was also true. Isn't that what all the addicts do?

Situations such as these caused me to reflect, but it was very difficult to change. Sometimes I spent time thinking about ways to quit the habit. I tried , but like those suffering paralysis, I was powerless; I lacked the strength to get out of the addiction.

Another incident that made me reflect and got me to stop crack for several days, involved my mother and Maria, her young friend and bingo companion, if I remember correctly. I came back home after several days of consuming drugs without eating any solid food. I was smoking one of the last rocks, when I sensed that someone was opening the door with a key. Paranoid, I hid everything quickly. But I didn't make it to the door in time to secure the chain lock. The door opened, and there stood my mother. Seeing her brought on so much shame that I wanted to hide. I began to run, but when I reached the kitchen, Maria grabbed me by the waist.

"Ay, hijo. Ay, hijo," mother cried repeatedly with great grief.

"Let me go! Let me go!" I yelled at Maria.

While I was trying to cut loose, we both fell to the floor.
"Juanita, don't cry. Salvador is going to be a Christian and a pastor," she yelled from the floor, almost leaving me deaf.

We calmed down. I went to the bedroom. I respected my mother very much. I saw her as the best person in the world because of her love. As soon as I could, I left the house thoughtful and full of shame. Why not become a Christian? After all, Christians are the only ones who have peace in this world. I will never forget the peaceful countenance of Damian, who had converted after being in prison in Bordentown. I meditated on this. I knew that it would be good for me to change. But I was dominated by drugs, like an ox by the yoke.

# A life for a smoke

We smoked at Joe's and Jenny's, Kenny Kent's sister's house, another den for crack heads, on 142nd Street. Although we had enough processed stuff on a little table in the midst of ten men and women, when everybody was high, we began looking obsessively for a little rock of crack we thought had fallen to the floor. It was incredible , but this would happen a lot.

"Stop looking for that stupid little rock. It probably didn't even fall."

We continued smoking. "Don't you guys realize...?" one of the new crack heads would start to complain.

"Shutup!" another would interrupt. "I saw it fall around here somewhere."

"I just gotta know: Why do we have to smoke with our guns in our hands? We might shoot somebody by accident? Why are we so uptight?" complained Israel, one of the guys that had a spot in the vicinity of 130 something, as we would say.

"You're going to have to kill me while I'm shooting," I said, laying my M1 short rifle across my legs as I held the smoky pipe in my hands.

The moment that we ran out of stuff, I went out with Mon to visit my friend Pupi, who had a spot close by. When we didn't find him, we got desperate. Mon signaled me to follow him. We entered a small business and he took his gun out. He demanded all the money. Then he forced the businessman to go to the back of the store, where we tied him up with his own rope and left him. We went back and smoked the meager take.

I did not like robbing business people. First of all, they were honorable citizens who had the right to report the robbery to the police. Secondly, the take was always less. You could always get more by robbing a drug dealer or gangster. Besides all that, I would feel less guilt robbing someone I believed was doing wrong themselves.

The fact of the matter is we robbed a lot of people of both types and sometimes we hit an unintended target.

I recall walking down a dark street during very early morning hours with three other outlaws. Someone had pointed out a guy to us and told us he was carrying a great amount of cocaine. We went after him. We reached him near 160th and Fort Washington. Once we got near the man, who was accompanied by a woman, I politely asked him for a match to light a cigarette I had in my left hand. As he reached into his pocket for the match, I took out my knife and quickly put it to his throat. I asked him to hand over the drugs in street language. From the look on his face, I saw he didn't have the slightest idea what I was talking about. He was no dealer. He was not a street man. Felipe checked him from head to toe, as we always did, to take any weapons or valuables he might have.

We started to run back to Mon's car, several cars away. The gentleman we had tried to rob had a gun in hand. I began to run. Then he opened fire with boldness and precision, wounding me on my side. He continued shooting, but I ran swiftly and desperately until I reached Broadway. I hailed a taxi and then, although I lost a lot of blood, was able to get myself to the hospital.

Later, I found out that the gentleman was a police officer. He had a complete right to come after me full force. But he didn't. He forgave my offense, which I considered to be a miracle.

Felipe, Mon and another young man, escaped without a scratch that night. However, some days later, death came to Mon in another incident. He was a man entrenched in street life. Hardened criminals respected him at first sight. He was a straight shooter, not one to pretend or try to fool people. But after he became addicted to heroin and cocaine, he would risk his life for a bag of "manteca"(heroin) or a "pipazo" (dose of crack). So his days were shortened. The last day I saw him, I said: "Be careful, because there are rumors that people are looking for an occasion to shut you up." He was a very self-assured man. I don't recall him answering back one word. The next day, the news arrived that Mon, along with other two guys from the block, had been assassinated in a very calculated and violent way.

In the midst of all this, we still did not learn the lesson. One tragedy after the other happened. Late at night they sent someone to me for a gun, because a spot with the highest sales had no protection. Because of the family ties between Forty Seven and the owner of the spot, who had also helped me in time of need, I loaned the apartment manager the "fuca," (which is what we called the gun.) Forty Seven had been arrested but would be released in a few days.

We returned at the agreed time in the early morning to pick up the "fuca" but they asked us to return in one hour. When we came back, no one was in the apartment. So I ordered someone to go in through the window. Once inside, we didn't find the gun. Kenny Kent, who had been one of the first to become wealthy selling heroin in the block, and who also had fallen into addiction, said he would take the television as collateral. We had no reason to doubt him.

I went home to sleep. I had been on the street for three days and was exhausted. When I returned to 158th Street, which became the new place we would go to, I was informed that Kenny had been kidnapped and rumors said he had been tortured and killed at the same spot last night. This was very painful for me as it was for the guys in the block. Kenny was very loved. We had known each other before becoming criminals. Our relationship was full of happy memories. I and others from the block armed ourselves and vowed to take revenge.

# 10
## ARRESTS

The deeper into criminal life you get, the more confusing it becomes as you cover your actions with lies and you lose track of which crimes you're being arrested or tried for at any given point. My memories of this season of my life are a blur,though the consequences are still very clear to me.

One night, while Forty Seven and I were coming out of a taxi on 158$^{th}$ Street, a friend that we called Black D, who was a hustler and a crack head, tried to be funny by announcing that "the stick-up kids" had arrived. Forty took offense and slapped him. The manager of an influential spot stepped out of the crowd and declared that we really had become a menace to everyone. I wanted to get into it with him right there, but the others held us apart. So Forty and I made up our minds that this insult would cost them all dearly.

We went up to the roof, leaving two of our guys to watch the stairway. We took a rope and tied it to a tube. Forty Seven tied the rope onto himself while I secured it and controlled it from the other end of the roof. I slowly lowered him toward the floor where this man's spot was located.

Suddenly, I lost my balance. I was weak and thin because of my addiction. I thought my friend's hour had come. I held on as long as long as I could, thinking that in the worst-case scenario it would be better for me to let him fall six floors than for me to be pulled off the roof. The rope threatened to split because of the pressure. But Forty Seven proved to be agile enough to get his feet onto the window ledge and get into the apartment. We took the weapons and over an ounce of cocaine that was there.

# Surprised by the police

At about noon the following day, Picky Louis and I went to 163$^{rd}$ to run a quick errand and return to an apartment that we used to have on 167$^{th}$ Street. We called this apartment "The Fortress." We had a guard watching the door with a machine gun hanging from his shoulder. We did not like surprises and avoided them at all costs. Many people said of us *"están calientes"* (they're hot). As we were leaving that street, someone approached us and said there was a client in the area that was looking for "something good" but wasn't happy with what he'd been shown. When he said he was looking for a minimum of thirty grams, we decided to sell to him. I had about an ounce and half and needed some cash. We waited for the client inside a building. Once inside the hallway, he asked to see the cocaine.

"Let me see what you have," he demanded, sounding like he was used to spending a lot of money on drugs.

"If you buy an ounce at regular price, I'll let you have an extra gram for free," I proposed.

"Treat me a little better. I'm a serious buyer," he said, flashing a large roll of bills.

A few minutes passed by. I never liked to negotiate in public like that. So I made a last offer. "Look. Apart from selling you the quantity you request at a good price I'll let you have a second free gram. Take it or leave it."

"What's all the pressure cousin?" he answered in a sarcastic tone, stalling the close of the sale.

He didn't change his attitude even when I took out a gun and pointed it at his head. Picky Louis also aimed at him from the small door that lead to the far end of the building. Suddenly, an armed policeman entered, weapon drawn, yelling:
"Drop your gun to the floor.

"Hey!" the client yelled when I gave him a big push in the direction of the policeman.
By that time we were negotiating close to the small door. I ran through it. At that moment I could see a way to escape, so I threw the .38 nickel gun as far as I could. I hid with Picky behind one of the building's walls. From the small door the police officer yelled: "Come out with your hands up".

Later, at the police precinct we were charged with possession of firearms. They checked me but couldn't find the cocaine I still had on me. While the police filled out paper work, Picky and I began breaking the cocaine rocks into dust. Then we put the dust into cigarettes, and while one smoked the other watched, right in the cell next to the police officers. We stopped just before I fell into a deep state of hallucination. Afterward, Picky's mother-in-law came to the precinct and we gave her a part and kept the other to continue with our jail cell "rumba", until we arrived at Rikers Island.

# Bigger risks, smaller returns

My bail was set at one thousand dollars. My lawyer came to pick me up. We began smoking together in the taxi. Arriving in Manhattan, he said goodbye advising me to be careful. I reached the neighborhood, my apartment on 139$^{th}$ St.. I was about to lose it. I hadn't paid the rent for two or three months. Sussy, the woman who lived with me at that time, had convinced the judge to give us some time to pay or move. I decided to run the risk of passing by 158$^{th}$ St. expecting to meet the guys. Sussy did everything possible to stop me from going.

We fought about it but I was so anxious to get into the streets that I resented all her efforts. It was still autumn and it wasn't cold enough to put on the long coat under which I usually carried my M1 rifle, so I took the chance of going out unarmed, since I had tossed my pistol before the arrest.

I arrived at 158$^{th}$ Street. A man with the manners of a refined gentleman was in from another state selling new guns he had brought. Once inside the hallway, which was infested with drug spots, he passed me a .38 caliber. I said that judging by its size and thickness, it looked more like a .44. I asked him to let me try a .38 bullet to convince myself. He agreed. Then I took the bullet and placed it in one of the six chambers of the barrel. I quickly rotated it until it was in a firing position. I pointed the gun at him and said I would keep it. He regretted trusting me. I told him I couldn't walk around unarmed and because I had just gotten out of jail I didn't have the one hundred fifty dollars he asked for the gun. I asked him to give me some time. At that moment I saw an unknown client going into a spot to buy. I took one hundred twenty five dollars from him and gave it to the gun salesman along with some cocaine.

My cash flow was sporadic. I did have some people paying me old debts. I also found at home, inside the mattress of my bedroom, a roll of twenty-dollar bills adding up to a thousand dollars. We used to stash money like that when times were good. So, we found lesser quantities in suits, drawers and other places. Finally, an old clock that a friend sold to me at a fairly low price, turned out to be the jewel in the crown at some eight thousand dollars. I used it to make a deal for cocaine with Oggy, who had the main spot on 158$^{th}$ St. My addiction became greater every passing day until I had to sell my fur coats, clothes and anything of value in the house. As time went by we lost the apartment. I moved to 158$^{th}$ Street, which by then had replaced 163$^{rd}$ Street in drug trafficking.

One morning I was smoking crack with Leo el Quimico and a friend in an apartment on the first floor, where I had moved office equipment I still had. Suddenly, someone pounded on the door and yelled: "Police! Open up!" I ran toward the window. I climbed out without thinking I was at a height of about nine feet, and jumped. I fell into a dumpster. My female friend also jumped and fell right on top of me. We ran like crazy from that place. We avoided arrest but I was in severe pain for several days.

On another occasion, I was in that same apartment with Leo. After smoking for a long while, I sniffed several bags of heroin, and like the lion after it eats a goat, I fell asleep on a mattress that was lying on the floor, with Sussy. Leo fell asleep shortly before we did, after telling us the story of how he had become a very powerful man, before I had even thought about becoming a criminal.

"Get up!" yelled a voice. Groggy, I felt a strong pressure on my chest.

"What's happening?" I asked, frightened. I could now see a police officer standing over me and yelling at me with one foot placed heavily on my chest.

"Where is the rifle?" he asked, as more officers swarmed into the apartment..

"What rifle are you talking about? I don't live here. I'm an addict. I only fell asleep here." I said, struggling to get the words out because he still had me pinned with his foot.

Sussy tried to object but they slapped her in the face, causing her to fall to the floor. They tried to wake Leo, shaking him roughly.

"Tell me, where is the rifle?" one of the officers insisted, the rest echoing his question.
Suddenly, someone who seemed Latino approached me.
"Look here, at your stupid rifle. Look at it! Look at it!" he yelled at me, shaking the rifle in my face, and kicking me repeatedly with rage.
"I've never seen that rifle in my life," I lied, faking innocence.
"You'll have to tell that to the judge," a second one threatened me, as a third picked me up roughly from behind and slapped handcuffs on me.

When we came out of the building, cuffed, I saw many police cars. As they were taking us to the 30th Precinct, I wondered how they had gotten into the apartment unnoticed. Later, I discovered that Chilly Willie, one of the guys who hung out with me, had been caught leaving another apartment and entering the one in which I'd been sleeping. Forty Seven and several others were also arrested at another part of the building.
Once we were in the precinct, the officers were laughing, enjoying the great arrest. I could hear some of them recounting the action. One, who seemed to be the unit's clown, was telling the story like a joke.

"These hoodlums are so bad, I had to punch one of them right in the pit of the stomach so hard that he went in his pants. We had to give him some time to change, but even with that he still stunk up he car. Filthy rotten addict!" The policeman scoffed, while I listened from my cell. His partners were enjoying the moment, celebrating with a concert of chuckles. The truth is he had good reason to laugh. I laughed, too.

During interrogation they told me that the reason I was arrested was that several people had complained that I was terrorizing them with my rifle. They proposed that I sign a confession of illegal possession of a firearm, so that the judge would be more lenient with me. They persuaded me to talk, so that the "lady" who was arrested with me could be released. Once in court, however, the judge voided my arrest because he said the police had forced entry to the apartment without a court order, and, furthermore, such a warrant would not have applied to me since I was no relation to the tenant.

## Addiction destroys youth

I tried to quit drugs more than once. But just like the spider web entangles its victim, so did my addiction every day, until my life was consumed. My mother was very thin and emotionally affected by the situation. I felt very bad about that. One night, I went with her to stay at the house of the stepsister I had grown up with, my stepfather Delfin's daughter. When I arrived, my nephew Junior, who was probably about three or four years old, was traumatized. He refused to come near me because he didn't want to see his *"tio feo."* (ugly uncle.)

I submitted to my mother's request that I begin a drug rehab program. But it took so much time the complete the paperwork that I became sick with symptoms of withdrawl. In my desperation, I excused myself to go the bathroom and went, instead, to 170<sup>th</sup> Street and Amsterdam, to the Highbridge pool park, which at that time was the spot for heroin. The park was teeming with young people; it seemed like an ant farm. Clearly, drugs were destroying the youth of the eighties.

# Rape and Revenge

A short time later, a young girl we affectionately called Shorty arrived, terrorized , at our new apartment on 158<sup>th</sup> Street. In a state of agony she told us that two men had raped her on a rooftop after leaving a spot. We rushed like lightning to the place. The porter didn't take our guns from us as they did with other visitors. The owner came out and welcomed us with respect.

"What happened with Shorty, *loco*?" I asked pleasantly because I knew him to be an honest man.

"I know that something happened, but I really don't know the whole story," he said while inviting me to sit down.

"Stop right there. Nobody move," yelled Chilly Willie and Forty as they disarmed the two workers.
"What's this Salvador?" asked the owner, surprised, as he got to his knees.

"I want you to know this is not a killing. We have come to reason," I assured him. "Shorty came here to buy *un buche*(some cocaine)and was abused."

We spoke as gentlemen. He explained that everything

had started at his spot but had ended away from there. He didn't have rapists among his men. So he promised to deliver the perpetrators. I asked him to send seven grams to Shorty to calm her down until we were able to avenge her. So he did.

# Hearing Sounds at Nani's Den

We went back to console Shorty at Nani la Negra's apartment. This apartment had been converted into a den for the crackheads of 158$^{th}$ Street, just like Joe Blow's at 163$^{rd}$ St. and Jenny Kent's at "130 something," which was really 142$^{nd}$ Street.

We were surprised to find her so strengthened. She had a good reason. She had taken advantage of the carelessness of one connection and had swindled a big quantity of cocaine. Losing no time, we took out numerous jars with water and baking soda. The torches were lit up. While the cocaine was cooking, we could hear the crackling sound of the stones that were put in the hot pipe. We looked like vultures attacking newfound corpses.

Nani, as always, would tell me I was the master of her house. We got along very well. We all felt comfortable there. After smoking crack for several hours, a very sociable woman who appeared to be rich arrived. After a while, she too smoked; she stared at me in the eye and began to talk.

"You speak like a preacher," she said softly, almost musically, while placing the pipe on my lips, which were now totally whitened by the smoke from pure cocaine exposed to fire.

"I have to go. If you come with me, I will give you all you want," she said, waiting for an answer.

"This woman has a thing for Salvador," some reacted.

"Bi, go and get cured. That old lady is filthy rich," said Forty in Spanish so that the woman could not understand.

I rejected her proposition. The girls kept talking about the shamelessness of the woman who had propositioned me. But I was quiet, was trembling on the inside because her words made me recall other times at which people had said I was a preacher. She left, and we kept smoking.

Then came my young friend, Sweepy, whom I had trained to work weighing materials during the time that Mr. Dandy and I distributed cocaine. We smoked until we began hearing strange sounds. Once again, we started hunting for imaginary rocks of crack on the floor, although there was plenty on the table. I kept hearing sounds.

"Your life is a book," said Nani.

"Why do you say that, *prieta*?" I asked her affectionately while I kept looking for the stone.
I stopped abruptly. "Everybody, quiet! I hear police radios! They're coming from the precinct to break down this door," I said, as I signaled for absolute silence, reached for a glass, and placed it against the wall so I could hear more clearly what was on the other side.

"You're spoiling the mood with your fears," Sussy rebuked me.
"Be quiet. You're jealous," I yelled. "Hide the weapons. I clearly hear police radios indicating this address." I said it firmly until they obeyed me.

At that moment, police pounded on the door. Our eyes were already bulging from cocaine abuse, but now they opened even wider in astonishment.
"Police. Open the door."

"Please come in," said one of us, who opened the door. The rest of us faked calm.

Detectives came in. One approached me.

"This pipe is yours. Come on answer! Is this yours?" he said, holding the pipe in one hand and his gun in the other, looking at each one of us.

They all gathered in the living room. They asked us if we sold drugs in that apartment. We said no. I stated that I was only an addict. They broke some of the pipes they were able to find. As they were leaving, one of the officers saw that mine was at the base of the sofa were I was sitting. He took it and while he walked toward the door, he turned around and threw the pipe in my direction angrily, breaking it at my feet.

# Night Shootings and Gang Wars

Hallucinations became more frequent every time I smoked. Many people did not want to smoke with me because I was always seeing and hearing strange things, usually with my pistol in my hand. It's true that saw or heard unusual things, but many of them turned out to be real.

I was smoking at home with Forty Seven. It was windy. The night was cold and dark. It was about three o'clock in the morning. Suddenly, a high-pitched scream was heard. I was convinced that someone was being tortured. I signaled to Forty Seven to listen. He pointed upward, confirming that he heard something coming from over our heads.

"Bi, let's check it out. Let's see what's going on," he whispered.

"I'll tell you. Someone is being tortured," I said in a similar tone.

As we started up the stairs, a large man was coming down with such speed that we had to let him pass. He passed by swiftly, notably aggressive. When we reached the fouth floor, we pushed open the door to Mike Moreno's apartment. He was laying on the floor in a pool of blood, moaning. The appearance of his face was monstrous; it looked like pounded meat.

Suddenly, I heard someone kick the door down. Forty Seven was after the supposed villain who, according to Mike, was a collector for the black gang. Mike was one of those salespeople that hadn't paid his debts. For that reason he got more than a half hour of torture at the hands of a fierce, cold strong man who measured five feet 11 inches and weighed about 220 pounds.

Mike, on the other hand, was of a medium build and the crack abuse, malnutrition and frequent lack of sleep had turned him into an old man prematurely. In spite of this, there was something good about him. His condition did not affect the characteristic he had that won the hearts of even the toughest men like my friends and I. Mike had the smile of a child that was very inconsistent with street life.

Leaving Mike in the care of one of the guys, I ran toward Broadway, driven by a spirit of vengeance. As soon as I was across the street from "The Monarch," a bar frequented by local gangs, I saw Forty Seven and another friend exchange blows with the collector that had beat Mike up. I yelled at Forty Seven to step aside.

Indifferent to the screams and cries of those coming in and out of the bar, I took out my .38 and fired two shots in a row.

The man fell to the ground twisting and moaning. Suddenly other shots were heard behind me. I positioned myself behind a car. Everybody ran. In the middle of all this confusion and shooting, police sirens were heard. Moving in a zigzag fashion between the cars parked across from and to the right side of the bar, I tried to scurry away from the patrol cars, which had multiplied like flies. Between the lights and sirens, I ran and met up with the other guys who quickly got hold of a getaway vehicle.

Frankly, we cared little what we left behind. Our hearts were hardened. Violence was just another adventure. We were street men, Satan's puppets. We had three functions: kill, steal and destroy.

Later, Mike informed me that the man I had confronted belonged to the same dangerous gang as two other men with whom I had had run-ins. They began hunting me down.

I had already taken a drug shipment away from one member. Another, I had ambushed in a stair well , demanding his drugs, money and gun. He resisted, shouting that if I climbed one step toward where he was, he would throw himself out of the open window to his left. I tried to convince him that if he jumped he could die, but as soon as I took my first step, he jumped. There was a tremendous scream followed by the slam when he hit the ground. The ambulance took him to the hospital, and he ended up in a wheelchair with severe complications. So they decided to get rid of me.

## Saved by Another Arrest

A few days after the incident with Mike's attacker, I surprised a member of the same gang who was trying to set a trap for me. He escaped me but I knew that now, more than ever, I had to watch myself.

But my addiction made me careless. I had so many enemies at that time that I wouldn't dare go alone anywhere. But I wasn't really keeping very good company or making wise decisions in "business" or in life.

Mr. Dandy returned from the Dominican Republic and proposed to let me have half of an eighth, which is sixty-two and a half grams, and even to smoke it with me if I promised to quit crack and commit myself to the business. I said that I wouldn't dare. He insisted. We smoked what he offered with two girls from our block. However, by the time he received the ten kilos of cocaine he was waiting for, I was out of business and headed for Rikers Island.

Forty Seven and I had begun dealing with people who had winter clothes to sell in exchange for money and cocaine. The transaction was frustrated. So was I. They started back toward their truck with two supermarket carts full of clothes. I pointed at them with a short barrel shotgun and demanded that they leave the clothes where they were or their lives would be endangered.

One or two days later, I smoked a crack so strong that I had to go outside the apartment to take a breath of the early evening air. I placed the shotgun under the stairway; I still had the humming in my ear that is produced by a high dose of cocaine. On my way out, I stopped by Nani's house. Showing concern, she asked me to leave the block because she feared I would be arrested. I quickly left her house; I needed some fresh air. Some guys were playing cards across the street behind the building, enjoying the outdoors. I approached them as they were preparing to give out the cards. I took the cards and shuffled them. I got ready to take out a card to "see what my luck was." I took out the king of clubs, which is the number thirteen and I said, "Ok, guys I'll see you. Today isn't my day." I lit a cigarette.

I stepped forward and heard a masculine voice from behind me. "Excuse me, sir. what's your name?"

I turned and gave him a name I don't remember.

"Don't you have another name?" asked a second man behind me, shining a flashlight in my face. Then another man approached me and asked me to accompany him to the 30th Precinct.

They put me in a lineup with other suspects. I was chosen. When I came out, a police officer patted me on the back with the palm of his hand and said: "Congratulations, you've won the first prize." I was identified as the perpetrator of an armed robbery. I would not see the streets of New York for almost three years. Prison: quick entry, slow exit.

# 11

# BEHIND BARS

Two police officers took me from the cell in the 30th Precinct, cuffed me and took me to Central Booking. Once my arrest had been processed they put me back in another holding cell. I began to feel the discomfort of heroin withdrawl. I lay underneath a bench, but couldn't find a comfortable position with my hands cuffed. I had no cigarettes. I was very cold. I was in a bad mood. I was sick. I sent the night in transit from Central Booking to a central precinct and finally to court. I rolled from side to side on the van floor.

We traveled inside a small police truck, which we called: "La Perrera" (The Dog Pound). About ten of us, mostly black and Hispanic, were being transported.

We were all shackled to one chain by the hands and fettered together at our feet. After smoking a cigarette butt, which I had begged from a prisoner down the line, I began falling asleep and nodding my head. The prisoner in front of me kicked me and yelled in my ear: "Listen! You're pulling my chain!" At another time, I would have fought him, but I was too weak even to speak.

Once we were in the "bullpen," as we called the cell where we waited to go to court, I fell on the floor, overcome by back pain. I didn't even care that I was lying on a dirty floor full of crumbs, mustard stains, and cigarette butts and ashes. Like a cowboy had hallucinating in the desert who imagines he sees a cool, shady oasis, I saw this filthy floor as a bed in a five star hotel. Exhausted and sick with heroin withdrawl,I fell asleep again.

I woke with a start when the guard called for a prisoner to see the judge. "Antonio Jimenez", he said, clearly and with good pronunciation, going from one cell to the next with his instructions in hand.

"Antonio Jimenez!" he repeated, raising his voice, slightly angry. When there was no response, the rest of us began to get impatient. "That Antonio Jimenez won't let me sleep," I complained. But then I recognized the name.

It was one of mine. I had forgotten that I gave the guard my uncle's name, Reverend Antonio Jimenez.

When the guard passed my cell again, I asked him: "Officer, are you calling for Antonio Jimenez? That's me," I said stepping up to the cell gate, embarrassed.

The judge set bail and they took me to the prison at Rikers Island, commonly known as "La Roca" (The Rock). The inmates also called it "La Isla" (The Island). At that time, it was said, about 12,000 inmates lived in the various buildings on "The Rock."

## Sick man in cell C-95

When we entered the cell for new prisoners at building C-95, I was aching all over. Wally and Poison, prison friends, greatly encouraged me. We ate together. I drank a hot beverage. Then I rested for a while on a bench and they both sat next to me to talk.

"They say you were busting heads out on the streets," Wally said.

"Behind bars again for cocaine and heroin," I lamented.

"The truth is he went to Africa to hunt some gorilla," Poison laughed, keeping his eye on the other prisoners.

Then another prisoner came over to show us a newspaper story and photo about the Young Blood case. It said a young man had pushed his mother through the window off of fifth or sixth floor while she was ironing because, under the influence of a drug called "angel dust", he thought she was a witch casting evil spells on him.

"Take a good look at the picture Dominican," said a prisoner who knew me from one of my former trips to prison.

"Look, Bi, it's that guy over there," Poison exclaimed.

"If he killed his mother, he's a devil!" said some of the inmates.

"Let's beat him up so he learns," Wally said. "We'll have to rip off his gold chains and shoes, so the guards think that was the reason for the beating."

Inmates who wear tattoos usually have their backs done with one that reads "Forgive me mother." Mothers are the only ones who never forget their sons no matter how badly they behave. Mothers are the only ones who come to the visiting halls with packages of clothes, cigars, and money for food. In their honor — and, of course, for whatever valuables he had that would enable me to buy cigarettes and extra methadone — I worked up the nerve to join in.

We waited until the guard left his post and we launched an attack. We threw a jacket on him, covering his face, and ganged up on him. We looked like hyenas devouring a zebra.

— Captain! Captain! — he yelled at the top of his voice

while we punched and kicked him everywhere, and took all his possessions.

We knew we didn't have much time.

"Those damn Puerto Ricans are killing me" he yelled, rattling the bars of the cell gate.

"Guards! Get me out of here!" he kept yelling.

Shortly thereafter, guards and the officials began arriving.

"What's going on here?" asked one of the captains.

"Quiet! Calm down!," ordered the guards, as they opened the cell.

"Get that guy out of here. He's crazy," protested one of the other inmates.

A captain ordered the guards to take Young Blood out of his cell. They seemed unconcerned about what had happened to this young man. Apparently, they were aware that he had killed his own mother. It was a well-known case. It's also a well-known fact in prison circles that inmates themselves deal out punishment for certain crimes. This one was the first on the list, even before cases of rape of women or children. This was about the most loved human being to every prisoner: a mother.

Finally, we were taken from the holding pen to the infirmary. I was very sick. The nurse calmed me, encouraging me very sweetly not to despair. She resembled my mother and even acted like her.

"It seems to me you've lost a lot of weight," she suggested.

"Yes. If your scale is accurate, I've lost almost forty pounds," I answered.

"I don't understand why a young man as wise as you has fallen into such deep addiction," she said. "Furthermore, it appears you have a venereal disease and will need treatment for that," she informed me.

Finally, they gave me methadone and sent me to a dormitory in the substance abuse program. There an inmate gave me an extra dose of methadone. I fell asleep as soon as a bed was assigned to me. I awoke when the guard on duty pounded on my bed frame loudly and repeatedly. It was breakfast time. I had slept between twelve and fourteen hours!

While I was having breakfast, I saw many friends I hadn't seen for some time. We set a time to meet as soon as we were transferred out of the substance abuse program.

When I was transferred to the unit above, I went out to the courtyard we used for recreation. I saw some friends that helped me to get methadone in exchange for some of the profits of the articles we had taken from Young Blood.

It was a very cold afternoon. To my disadvantage, I didn't have a good jacket. I was arrested wearing a black leather jacket but no shirt; black pants and shoes but no socks. As soon as the bell sounded, I was one of the first to return to the unit. Now my body aches were worse. I practically froze in the courtyard. I drank a large dose of the unauthorized methadone I had procured. I fell asleep like a bear going into hibernation. I woke up at night. Most of the inmates were sleeping. I began a conversation with Villa Mella, one of the guys from my old neighborhood at 137th Street. There were also other prisoners talking. The guard ordered silence but we ignored him and continued talking. The guard returned.

"If you don't quiet down, I'll put you in the dungeon," he threatened.

"You and what army?" I answered.

The guard turned around to leave.

"I'll kick your behind," said another prisoner, imitating a female voice.

As soon as I began falling asleep, I was awakened by strong thumps on my bed.

"Captain, this is the wise guy," accused the guard on duty as other guards shone flashlights in my face.

"Get up!," commanded the captain.

They didn't give me time to get up. They grabbed me out of bed, and shoved me along out of the unit. Once I was out of the other prisoners' sight, they began punching and kicking me and pushed me into an unoccupied reception cell. I remained on the cold floor. The effect of my last methadone dose was wearing off. Once again I was feeling the pain of lack of heroin. I gave a lot of thought to the trap I had fallen into because of this addiction.

At the beginning, I hadn't liked the taste of heroin. I remembered vomiting the first time I got near it; my body was reacting naturally to prevent the dependency that now plagued me.

I thought about this until the break of the new day. The captain interviewed me. As a result of my infraction, I was transferred to a different unit and sent to the dungeon of another building, known as the blocks, a true human jungle.

## Dungeon or madhouse

The prison cells looked like bird cages lined up in a pet store, one row on top and one on the bottom. Of course, the thick steel bars were not as delicate as those on cages for birds. Someone mentioned my name while the guard led me to a cell. I heard the unpleasant sound of the dungeon gates locking. Alexis, another new prisoner, supplied me with reading material and cigarettes. From time to time we would exchange messages from cell to cell through an inmate we trusted who made the rounds making sure no one committed suicide.

A few days later, I was standing in the cell, holding on to the bars, smoking a handmade cigarette. There was a strong latrine odor.

"Hey, savage," Alexis called.

"Talk to me, partner," I answered.

"It looks like the crazy guy in the cell next to you is playing with his excrement again," he said, laughing.

Moments later, a captain and two guards arrived, yelling at my neighbor to use the toilet, not the floor. I didn't hear a word out of the prisoner. The next thing I saw was sudden stains on the captain's white shirt. He moved from side to side but it became increasingly difficult to avoid the crazy man's filth, which he was firing like ammunition from a machine gun. The captain and the guards left. The inmates were laughing hilariously. We yelled from cell to cell. For a moment we didn't care about the terrible smell. I though to myself that place was more of a madhouse than a dungeon. Sometimes, in the middle of the night, a scream was heard. On other nights, someone would sing a romantic song or say a poem out loud. The atmosphere was so crazy any one of us could have been driven to play with his own excrement. Contrary to the substance abuse program, which resembled a hospital, this dungeon seemed like a lunatic asuylum.

Suddenly, a warning interrupted my train of thought: "Freeze. They're coming back." Next, a deadly silence reigned. The air was filled with suspense. The captain and his guards stopped to my right, across from my neighbor's cell. They took a hose and began shooting water. All sorts of curses spewed from the mad man's mouth. I saw the water come out with so much pressure and for such a long time, that I asked myself if they were trying to kill him. The mad man screamed as the force of water began to inflict real pain. When it was over, silence permeated the cell block.

I had to go to court. The inmates were cuffed in pairs at both hands and feet. Many of us knew each other, but I'd never seen the partner I had this time. While forming a line to board the bus that would transport us to the courthouse, a friend greeted me.

"You won the prize. It's your turn, loco," he said smiling.

Suddenly, my partner threw a punch at me. We got into a fight and fell to the ground, hitting each other. The guards jumped all over us. They separated us and I saw a big guard sit on the crazy man and beat him into subjection. I breathed a sigh of relief when I was assigned a new partner.

## A punishment worse than prison

After ten days in the dungeon, I was transferred to block 6. Some neighborhood friends and other street acquaintances greeted me there. I was still sick with the back pain and other symptoms. I began an exercise routine, and to read and play chess. I stopped going to the Catholic Church because they expelled me and two other guys for irreverence. But I continued visiting the law library, not seeking my freedom or anybody else's, but to meet with friends that I would normally not see because of different activity schedules.

During that time there were about thirty young inmates from my neighborhood: Old Stick, Billy the Watchman, Felix, Johnny Chain, Johnny el Boricua, los hermanos Borbones, among others.

Many of us that had fought in the street would make

peace in jail. We got together and shared with those we trusted how we really felt. Many confessed that they were to blame for losing their wives, children and family. Others were steeped in bitterness at having been betrayed by crime partners. These fell into deep depression, fantasizing about executing the "traitors." Some expressed how convicted they felt for killing someone they weren't sure was guilty. This particular worry produces much insanity in jails. Little Mike, my friend from Columbus Avenue was accused of six murders and creating his own private cemetery in upstate New York. He said he didn't sleep well at night because "the dead scolded him for taking their lives." He said they would visit him and leave scratches all over his body.

I knew that penalties imposed by the two judges who tried my cases would not be only judgment I would suffer. As soon as I was alone, there would be an onslaught of mental images of the evil deeds I had one as well as pictures of the opportunities I had lost by choosing way of a life in the streets.

Why did I reject studying music, the path my father had asked me to follow? Why didn't I continue studying music? Why did I fall into these addictions that were nothing but dead ends? Why did I shoot that man, who was probably the father of a family? And what about his mother? How much did she suffer? Will I be a criminal all my life? If I weren't one, what would I do?

It was clear, guilt tortured me just the same as any other prisoner.

I remembered a picture painted by a prisoner that showed a man locked up in a cage with a little bird. In the picture the cage door is open and the man is inside, but his right hand is extended out through the door. In his hand, the bird is perched, wings spread, ready to fly.

The popular interpretation says that this picture symbolizes a man whose spirit is free in spite of the fact that his body is in prison. To me and many others, it is evident that the bird represents our conscience and our thoughts, which may physically leave a jail cell but, according to divine order, cannot bring back good news if it must harvest where evil has been sown.

My bird would be the bearer of my greatest torture: my mother remaining faithful even when I persisted in my unfaithfulness. I could literally hear my mother's cry on the day of my sentence. Her pain to me was greater than mine. She was the victim of a terrible deceit. From the time a mother carries a son in her arms, while breast-feeding him, she dreams to see him graduate as a doctor, an engineer or an attorney, etc. She never thinks someday he will become a criminal. This is how I destroyed my mother's dream. I became a street man, destined to visit three places: hospitals, jails, and cemeteries. I had visited the first two more than once. And given my persistence in the way of evil, I apparently didn't fear the third.

## Decidedly without direction

I received two concurrent sentences, two to six years and one to three years, to be served simultaneously. It seems there was someone in heaven that loved me very much. I was arrested for minor crimes. I was happy with the two minimum sentences. I knew very well that other people that committed lesser crimes than I received maximum sentences because they were arrested in the process of committing a major crime. Some received sentences of decades — or more. Little Mike, convicted of a very serious crime was in for one hundred ten years.

"Mr. Sabino, prepare your belongings. Tomorrow you are being transferred", the guard informed me interrupting my thoughts.

That morning we were about a hundred inmates waiting in our cells. We talked in small groups. The chatter was a mix of street stories, tales of other prison transfers, general complaints, and laughter for no apparent reason.

Then the sound of shackles and cuffs was heard as the guards in charge of transportation arrived. They threw the shackles and cuffs on the tables. They began calling name by name. They tied us. We came out of The Rock, but we didn't know where we were going.

We only knew we were going to a reception area, which was true. We arrived at Downstate Correctional Facility. The showered us with some chemicals. They gave us all the same hair cut and a numbered uniform. We were all forming a line following the same process: the single telephone call, the infirmary, the cafeteria, and television hour. Everything was synchronized. Everything was very well coordinated. Everything was very mechanically done, cold.

Two weeks later, we were called again. "Transfer," said the guard standing at the cell door. Again, very early in the morning, before sunrise, the sound of shackles and cuffs were announcing our departure.

"Officer, where are we going?" asked one of the prisoners as we boarded the bus.

"I'm not a social worker; I'm an officer," replied the guard without ever looking back at the prisoner.

"I think this road leads to Sing Sing," he whispered while I was traveling with my partner Speedy, from the Lower East Side of Manhattan.

We finally arrived at the old prison. It seemed to be abandoned. It was very dirty. But there was a certain sense of liberty. Friends whom we hadn't seen for a long time greeted us. Old Stick, who supplied me with cocaine when

I needed to satisfy my addiction, would also bring me some food. Others would give me clothes, toiletries, and marijuana. Home boys often clicks in prison to help one another. I began to feel comfortable at this prison but I knew I was only in transit.

That night, as soon as the bell rang and the iron doors shut with a clang, an officer ordered me to get ready for a long trip.

The bus ran for many hours. Talk among the inmates was: "We are going to such and such prison". The bus would stop at a prison, two or three would be dropped off, and we would continue our journey. We stopped at about four prisons. My group remained at the last one: Clinton Danemora Correctional Facility. I was about nine hours away from the city.

This did not keep my mother away at all. On the next visiting day she brought all the things I might need that were allowed by prison authorities. The meeting hall at Danemora was relatively peaceful. I quickly got into a routine. I spent a lot of time reading books and exercising. I always had lots of friends. In my unit, I would get together with a group of people from Harlem, from the Lower East Side, from my neighborhood and other city ghettos.

Johnny T.V., one of the long-time Washington Heights criminals, was the oldest of us at around 50. Some of the prisoners opposed my relationship with him. They were looking for an opportunity to attack him because he had been the ringleader in the killing of eight young men who had risen up against him and attacked one of his puntos. After listening to opinions from different sources, they decided to leave him alone.

During the month of June, when softball started, we headed for the courtyard enthusiastically. Two of the players were discussing who was going to bat first. One of them, whom I met through a friend, asked me to lend him the bat I had so he could beat up the guy that was not letting him bat first.

"Look, let me borrow your bat to hit this guy in the head," he asked quietly, reaching for the bat.

"That's not right. He asked to be up first. He goes before you. Let him finish," I proposed.

"Let go of the bat," he insisted, yanking it from my hands with all of his strength.

When I yelled back at him to stop, he punched me in the chest. I jumped on him like a wild animal. We fell to the ground fighting. I heard the sentinel's voice echoing from the tower's loudspeaker. The inmates were also yelling at the top of their voices. Suddenly, I felt someone attack me from the back. I grabbed his legs and he fell to the ground. I heard people talking to me. It was the guards separating us. The man who had fallen to the ground was also a guard! They cuffed us and pushed us all the way out of the patio. Then we were sent directly to the dungeon.

## Prison is a small world

After coming out of the dungeon I returned to normal. We had fun cooking our own food, participating in activities like running, playing softball, and other games such as chess, dominoes or cards. In addition, each inmate had to work in some type of workshop. I worked in the carpenter's workshop. Additionally, every inmate had religious options. After about eight months, I was transferred to an institution closer to New York City.

The Mid Orange correctional facility presented a totally different setting. It was made up of six residential cabins, plus bigger buildings like the auditorium, cafeteria, workshops, classrooms and the gym, which at that time had a swimming pool.

When I arrived, there was a fight going on between two groups over drug transactions, mainly involving marijuana and cocaine.

"El Bambi is a good guy, but he's all by himself. He needs help, Sal," said an old friend. "With some help from us, everything will be alright. I don't like the abuse that goes on here. That group over there is perverting the Latino minors."

"What do mean by that?" I asked.

"They have a small kid that washes their clothes and serves as a woman for the leader," he said.

Some days later, we were exercising, after speaking with Bambi, and they pointed out to me the main guy of the opposing group.

"Hey fatty, your tummy is growing," I laughed at him.

"Where do you know me from?" he asked, as I approached him.

"I don't want you here. You stink. Get out of here! And say the same thing to the bums that hang out with you." I threatened him while he took note of the big group that was with me.

After a few minutes, Yuyin arrived. He was one of the neighborhood guys who had been in prison for twelve years for multiple homicide.

"Why do you come in here sounding the war cry? El Bambi is another problem person; watch your back," he advised. Others intervened. Two or three guys from the opposing group who knew me decided to help work out a peaceful solution. It worked and things were under control for a while.

But the place became more and more corrupt because both groups continued to get more involved in bringing drugs into the prison.

One Christmas Eve, Forty Seven and Sweepy arrived at my unit. I was smoking marihuana in the bathroom. We didn't know how it happened but all of sudden the guard on duty was standing in front of me while I was sitting on the toilet smoking.

"Mr. Sabino, what are you doing?," he asked.

"Sorry, officer, it's Christmas. We are all very sad." I made excuses for myself while throwing the rest of the marijuana in the toilet and flushing it.

He invited me to the office. He proposed that I throw away the entire drug load I had in exchange for his silence. I didn't do exactly what he asked me to do, but we made no more trouble while he was on duty.

Just like drug dealing in the streets, prison drug dealing caused daily problems. Many of the prisoners bought cigarettes and food to exchange for drugs when they were available. They amassed cash to buy large quantities of drugs. Wherever there are drugs, violence will increase.

Our group felt very safe because we had the reputation of being well armed. In addition, each time the prison bus arrived, it brought more friends from the streets.

When someone from our block arrived, we would supply them with the things they needed: protection, cigarettes and drugs.

When a confrontation among different groups of the MidOrange prison seemed it was about to explode, the guards invaded our unit. They went directly to the place where our group hid the weapons. They found eleven weapons in a superficial raid. We came to the conclusion that we had a "rat" in the house; therefore, after a brief interrogation we prepared for vengeance. I set a meeting with the first suspect in the kitchen of the unit where I cooked. Mustafa had the appearance of an African prince. He didn't need to fear anyone. He was tall, strong and very popular among his group. No one would have wanted to be his opponent. I had no alternative. He didn't like us and it was inconvenient for him that my group had such power in the unit we were forced to share. I asked Forty Seven, Sweepy and Colombia to cover me, and watch for the police or any intruders.

"What's happening?" asked Mustafa, sitting on a wooden bench.

"Why did you do it?" I accused him, pointing my index finger at him and showing my anger.

"How dare you....?"

I didn't give him a chance to say anything. The streets had taught me that in a fight, surprise is better than strength. Suddenly, I began punching him all over. I took out a little jailhouse knife. He ran toward the door. He escaped through it while I was stabbing at his back.

Tension escalated higher than before. Another suspected of turning us in was one of the most influential leaders of Mustafa's group. Bushwick had lost control of the unit. So he tried to take advantage of one of the minors in our group. I arranged to meet with him in the washroom. At my instruction, the minor gave him one good hit, breaking his jaw so that he had to be hospitalized outside of the prison. They had to perform surgery on him and put him in traction for a long time.

Rumors broke out that someone who worked in the metal shop had given weapons to a second group that opposed us. We came to find out that our friend Colombia was the man. We were in the gym, boxing gloves on, taking turns hitting the punching bag. I decided to act.

"Colombia, we've been friends forever. Why do you give knives to those guys?" I asked.

"I made two knives for Barba Negra. He's not against us," he said, defending himself.

"I don't see how you and your friend could move thousands of kilos being such cowards. Forget our agreement. When I leave this place, I'm not moving one kilo with you. You might fall into the federucos' hands and crow like a rooster. You supplied our opponents with knives because they pressured you. Can't you see that every time something happens "Barba Negra" blames us? Are you stupid or a coward? I'm not going to stab you. Just put 'em up and fight."

"Way to go, Bi!" Forty and Sweepy said. "We run the place here. Just let anyone show up and raise his hand against us."

The tension grew higher in the unit. Everyone was on guard, measuring every step; no one went alone to the bathroom or the kitchen. Everyone was alert. Like cats ready to jump on prey, we were in attack mode. We knew some were very well armed. It was impossible to live under such tension. Something had to be done. We opted to lay the cards on the table. We waited for the guards on the second shift. The officer was skinny, careless, and a drunkard. We thought he was funny.

We summoned six of the more notorious leaders to a

meeting in the television room.

We tuned in to a boring show and pretended to watch it while we conducted our meeting.

"Now hear this," I announced. "I'll be in the bathroom. Anybody with the nerve or something against us, show up and fight – fists or weapons."

"The man has clearly spoken. Let's have the tough guys come out now or forever hold your peace," said Alex, a black man, standing to his feet at a height of five feet eleven and two hundred twenty pounds.

Sometimes I thought there was a death sentence on me. Even in my dreams, I would see myself handcuffed and sentenced again by a judge. If this were not torment enough, I also dreamed that the blue, sunlit sky turned completely red. The stars exploded and violently shook the firmament. The planets, satellites and other celestial bodies left their orbits and began careening wildly through space.

As the chaos increased, I noticed that the red color in the sky was that of blood and that the heavens were falling to the earth, which was now trembling under my feet. Suddenly, I saw myself as a ten-year old child, dressed in a black suit and a white shirt and tie. I was standing on a wooden pulpit, yelling to multitudes of people about their blindness; they didn't see what I saw: "The end is near. The world is coming to an end. This is the end. Jesus Christ offers you the last opportunity." All of a sudden, I woke up sweating, trembling on my little bed. My last scream still echoed inside the small room. Some time passed before I was able to get a hold of myself. I sat on my bed thinking: "I must be going mad. These types of dreams are constantly stalking me. Why do I dream this way?"

# Time's just taking its time

The routine continued. It seemed like my watch had frozen. Sometimes it felt like my release day was getting farther away from me. My thoughts ran wild, leaving me in fear and deep depression.I felt like I couldn't breathe.

When will I leave this place? Will I end up trapped in here like others who were even at less risk than I? There were those who'd been stabbed from behind, and were dead before they'd had a chance to realize what happened. Others had gotten AIDS when bitten during fight. Weren't my fears realistic? Could I ignore the possibility that my lady partners, living their own perverse lifestyles, could have been the victims of monstrous diseases?

I was a real tough guy when it came to fighting, mainly because I knew the odds were against me. But I didn't have the courage to face my own fears.

I worried about something happening before my release that would extend my sentence. I feared dying as an old man behind bars.

Time is a slow monster that weighs too much to walk. Like the turtle, the queen of slow, it seems not to move.

What if the parole board, after reviewing my case, added eight more months? The next time, I thought, the police will have to shoot me many times because I'm not falling behind bars for one more day! No way I'm going to be arrested again!

But in reality, who is going to stop the clock? Certainly the day is coming.

My mind raced in circles. Every day I ran from two to eleven miles on the track. Around and around. I would bend, stretch, exercise, sweat. I was determined to body build with the gym machines. Then Manny the pianist arrived. So did others, even a police officer that was a musician. Salsa rhythms were heard at every show and on jail festival days, which our families were able to attend. "Your trumpet will be very much missed. You'll be leaving soon," my partners said a little sadly during practice for the festival. They were really true friends. They made me reflect on the days when I had wanted to devote my life to music with all of my heart. They made me remember the beautiful moments when my friend Danny and I waited for my mother to go to work so we could play our trumpets from 8 a.m. to dusk. My teacher, Jerome, to whom Johnny Pacheco had referred me, came to play at the Happy Hills Casino with the youth orchestra "Los Intocables."

What a night it was! Trumpeters from everywhere! Bomberito Zarzuela and Nahum were playing. The experts competed among themselves. The youngest of us learned tricks to bring out a better sound, play higher notes, have more flexibility. How nice it was when Larry Spencer, Jerome Callet, Tony Penn and I played together a very popular jazz Latino rhythm! What a quartet! Now we could hear Danny, Jose Alberto "El Canario" (The canary) playing their salsa. But the moment was spoiled for me by the changes already happening in my life. I couldn't live on the salary of an average musician. I hardly dared get onto the stage. I feared being surprised by another Roberto Viralata, a hit man from my past who, if they hadn't stopped him, would have shot me right in front of a concert audience in George Washington High School.

# A vow to do better

The golden morning of the prison festival arrived. The sun was shinning. The mood in the jail was happy with the anticipation of the things which festivals bring: food, music and visits. The trumpets sounded announcing the beginning of the event.

When we were through with our set, I was talking to my visitors and keeping one eye on the guard that was watching. Benny gave the order: "Pass this to our partner."

His companion, a woman who looked like a model in one of those magazines that circulate in prison, began passing me the "stuff."

I signaled Forty Seven to help me take part of the "gift." It was a lot. "You're too much, partner," I said.

As soon as we returned to the unit, everybody took their places. One distracted the police. Another one watched the main door of the unit to make sure we wouldn't get a surprise visit from the sergeant on-duty. A third one was standing near the washroom door. And two more were pretending to use the bathroom. Forty and I were engrossed in emptying our bowels filled with cocaine, heroin and marihuana.

"I'm missing the last one," said Forty Seven, his voice strained. He steadied himself with one hand on the wall, standing up across from the bathroom sink, while he forced his intestinal muscles to push out the last package.

"There we go. You crazy hedonist!" I heard Sweepy praising him.

"Push, Sal. Bring it on! Forty already did his second round," said Sweepy, putting on the pressure.

We got everything ready quickly and did cocaine and

heroin from three in the afternoon until eleven at night. Now alone in my room, at the peak of my high, I began to do some thinking. Am I going to be an addict the rest of my life? Hadn't addiction "destroyed the empire," as an old friend used to say? So I thought the whole night without sleeping. The next morning, I got together with Sweepy and Forty Seven.

"I want you to hear me. My life is going to change totally. I thought all night about the people I let down because of drug addiction. I've gone through the biggest shame down to the last detail. While on the streets I begged and hurt people for a dose of crack. Four months and I'm out of here. And I can't go back to the same thing. I have made a radical decision. I will no longer mingle with drugs. I give any one of you permission if I fall again to kidnap and lock me up somewhere until I quit the habit. Even more, if you find me smoking crack, shoot me in the head," I said pointing at my forehead with my right hand and pulling an imaginary trigger. "If you want to continue with the addiction you will no longer be my friends. I will no longer hang out with addicts. I will sell, but will not consume anything," I said emphatically.

"Bi, I'm with you," promised Forty Seven
"You can shoot me, too," said Sweepy.
With firmness and determination I put my right hand on the table I used to paint stained glass. My friends' hands clasped over mine.

"Today, we vow never again to use drugs," I said, confirming our covenant.

We concentrated totally on physical exercise.
"You must be ready for the streets," said Nelson Muela. "It looks like you have a sixteen-inch arm. There won't be a girl that will resist you or a tough guy that will bring you down. You'll be out in the middle of summer.

The clock kept marking time. "Thirty days and one wake up," my friends counted with me every morning. "Twenty-nine, twenty-eight" and the days kept going by. Finally, the moment arrived: July 1st, 1985. Sweepy and I were escorted to the exit gate. The "Feds" cuffed Sweepy because he was in violation of immigration law. But I wasn't. Bambi was waiting for me with a gun, a woman, her drug of choice, and money to celebrate freedom my way.

# 12
## OPTIONS

I enjoyed seeing the neighborhood through he limousine window as the driver cruised the streets. Washington Heights was happy. It was summer. The sound of merengue was heard in the streets: "Baila en la calle de noche. Baila en la calle de dia." (Dance in the streets day and night.) The sun was scorching hot, the sound of the cars and people gathered on the sidewalks in front of their buildings, on the corners, and in the small parks along the middle of Broadway, boosted my mood. People played dominoes; others drank beer. Young men drove sports cars, stopping suddenly and screeching the tires. Dressed casually but in brand name clothes, they blasted their stereos at full volume amd flashed wide smiles under dark lenses. From time to time, they would shout flirtatious remarks, inspired by the eye-catching walk of one of the many women parading their sparkling beauty.

I meditated while watching life go on in the neighborhood. I was a free man again. I was aware of my abilities. I could make a living in many ways. I was very skillful in business. I could sell a space heater in the dessert, ice to an Eskimo and even dreams to dreamers. Obviously, I had other options. But I preferred the environment of the streets.

## It's never late to change.

I came out of the taxi across the street from Lento's

building. I entered the building cautiously. A young lady who was in the corner of the elevator wouldn't take her eyes off me. I asked her if she knew me. "You are a murderer", she said, pointing her finger at me, without blinking. "But you won't always be."

I was disturbed for a moment. My mind traveled at the speed of light. The elevator door opened and I followed her. She asked me to go away. She opened her apartment door and tried to close it in my face, but I held it open and asked her if there was a man in the house. She asked me to wait in front of the building and that someone would speak with me. I checked the Beretta .25 caliber pistol I carried.

"I know that you and my brother were great friends. You were with him the day he died. We expected you to take revenge on the culprits," said the emissary. I promised him that very soon everything would be resolved. After visiting Lento and making plans to begin "working" in August, I went to La Negra Nani's house. She greeted me with two of her friends. I spent the whole night with them buried in the multiple pleasures of my prison fantasies.

Then I returned home. I was ashamed of the way in which my mother and step father lived.
"Mama, get another apartment. I've got the money to move. Don't bother taking the old furniture. We can go to the store and buy everything new," I said, looking around in disgust.

"Oh, my son. Don't start selling drugs again," she begged and implored me.
"I don't know what else to do, mama," I yelled. "I'm too old. I need to take advantage of the time I have."

"You're a child. You have your whole life ahead of you.

You haven't turned twenty-nine yet. There are old men graduating as professionals every year," she insisted.

"It's too late for me. I have a criminal record. In fact, I don't even want to be a musician. I'll be a drug dealer no matter what happens," I said with determination.

"You can change. It's never too late to change," she said, crying. I went into the bedroom and lay down on the small bed like a scolded child.

# A new start, my way

After a month we had a meeting at Lento's house. I invited my friends Rony and Sweepy who had been released on bail from the Department of Naturalization and Immigration. We agreed to begin distributing cocaine, wholesale and in small quantities. Lento and I would work as partners, Sweepy and Rony would have a minimum salary that was somewhere around fifteen hundred dollars a week until the business improved. Porters and watchmen began at half that salary.

We began helping some friends move a shipment of twenty-five kilos they had received to work with a Colombian friend that was soon to arrive in New York with a bigger shipment. Three weeks later, business was booming. I contacted some big clients. Retail sales greatly multiplied. However, business problems inherent in successful drug dealing began. A neighbor, who distributed in the neighborhood, complained someone had stolen his "stuff" and that the thief was across from our building trying to find a way to do it to others. So I looked into the matter.

"Who are you waiting for, loco?" I asked, as I approached him.

"Take it easy, everything's fine," he said, calmly leaning on a car.

I threw a hook-punch to his left side leaving him total-ly out. I grabbed him by his belt from behind, picked him up and said to Sweepy, "Take this trash off our block," I took his car key and and handed it to Miriam, Benny's sister.

The dealers made an agreement to keep the heat — police attention — off our block. We put in effect a plan of zero tolerance for any public drug use. And we declared war on outsiders: thieves, intruders, informants, etc... Clearly, not all our rivals would allow themselves to be threatened by this. And I was aware that even some of our partners agreed to this territorial strategy only out of fear.

One night, I was on my way from 161st Street and Fort Washington toward my mother's apartment at 133rd and Amsterdam, and was passing 157th and Riverside Drive, at about 1 a.m. There was a soft breeze coming off the Hudson River and a view of the Garden State – New Jersey – on the other side. But I was disturbed. I told Chichi, the driver, that I thought we were being followed by one or two cars. He confirmed that they had been following us since shortly after we left. By that time, they had turned on the high beams and we could not see how many passengers were in each car. I ordered him that under no circumstance should he allow either of those cars to pass us, and that he should stop abruptly before reaching 150th Street, where there is a slight curve in the road. We reached that point and he stopped suddenly and turned left. We threw ourselves to the right side of the car, and got out with our guns drawn. The two drivers behind us also stopped short, turned around and peeled off in the opposite direction.

We got to my mother's building and entered. The hall-way was completely dark. I thought it probably didn't have anything to do with the people who were after us, but I took out my Browning as always. "Nobody moves or I shoot," I said when I heard a sound. Since it was couple from the building, I only asked them to remain against the wall until I passed.

We would mot stay long, since the place wasn't very safe for us. My mother thought that the virgin of Altagracia, illuminating the small living room with its electric lights and candles, was sufficient protection. Bambi's mother, who visited us for several days, trusted that her prayers to God guaranteed protection especially when trying to get others to become Christians.

One morning, she came into my room and kindly asked me not to deny her request. "Listen to this hymn, my son", asked Doña Isaura passing me a portable tape player. Only a heartless man could deny such a request from a sweet old lady. I lay back and listened to the song attentively.

*"Eran cien ovejas que había en el rebaño*
*Eran cien ovejas que amante cuidó*
*Pero una tarde, al contarlas todas*
*Le faltaba una, le faltaba una,*
*Y ESA ERES TU"*

*There were a hundred sheep in the fold*
*A hundred sheep He lovingly cared for*
*But one evening, at counting them*
*One of them was missing... one of them was missing,*
*AND THAT ONE IS YOU"*

As time went by I learned that the last line of the song really goes: "And     He     sadly     wep,t," referring to the love of Jesus the Good Shepherd for each one of us when we go astray. But instead of hearing "And     He sadly     wept", which is what the original tape says, I heard

Doña Isaura's voice saying, "And     t hat     one     is
you." The shepherd was really looking for the missing
sheep: Me.

# Predictions from spirits

My mother took me several times to a witch doctor. But
now she insisted that I make an appointment with Oggy's
wife. According to her, Oggy had almost been arrested on
several occasions but had escaped because of magic charms
done by his wife and other people that worked with her.
Since Oggy had found me an apartment in his building in
the Kingsbridge area of the Bronx, I made an appointment
with her. Her father was a "Baca" (a sort of ranking voodoo
witch doctor) who worked in connection with voodoo hier-
archy in Haiti. I went to several consultations.

It was determined that I needed everything from a bath
in herbs to a high priced protector from Haiti, for which I
would need to pay thousands of dollars.
"You will never land in prison", the "mysteries" pre-
dicted through two witches as they went into a trance. "Dee
mystery protact you from all evil," they would say in a
Haitian accent.

On Friday, October 25th as night was falling, I entered
the consultation room to the sound of bells ringing. There
were many pictures and illuminated statues, small candles,
large candles and other lighting that gave a mysterious glow
to the room. Everything seemed to be well prepared and
carefully arranged. I had also been very careful to comply
with everything they requested in detail. I had dressed in a
beige suit and burgundy color shirt, tie, belt and shoes. I
wore the best perfume. I had a bouquet of two-dozen of
partially opened red roses in my hands. The fire was flaming and clouds of smoke were coming from the burning

incense that announced her gala entry. Her dress was a bright blue contrasted by golden hems and folds. The multiple jewels, earrings, hoops, necklaces, bracelets, ornaments and rings, jingled in sensual rhythm with the movements of the approaching woman.

The whole room — set up as a sanctuary — was saturated with the aroma of that woman: The Mistress, to those who know the mysteries; Mitricili for the general public. Sniffing deeply, she smelled each and every rose until she had gone through the bouquet. I took the roll of hundred-dollar bills she had required and deposited it in the golden chest in front of her picture.

"Your engagement ring," she demanded, extending her left hand, passion in her voice and a direct sensual look in her face.

"Here it is," I said, in the tone of a movie actor, taking her hand with reverence to slide on the aquamarine ring.

"First this," she said, taking the ring and linking it with mine, which was of the same stone. She did it in a ceremonious way and placed them both in a very fine basin. After pouring in flower-scented water and other flammable aromatic substances she struck a match, and lit a fire. She put her hand in the flaming basin and took out the two rings in the middle of the fire. She stood up. We exchanged rings in front of the altar as a bride and groom. She hugged me and began kissing my face. She stopped for some seconds, only to stare at me with the penetrating and provocative look of a woman madly in love. Then, in slow motion, she approached me. She kissed my lips and whispered in my ear: "You are my groom."

Her farewell was as triumphant as her entry. The time

that I had anxiously awaited had arrived. All these scenes had been acted out for the benefit for "the mysteries"; now it was my turn. I was tired of preludes; I wanted the truth. The commitment I had made made me feel guilty because I felt such ceremonies should be reserved for a girl worthy of the honor. Still, I don't think I had ever tried to please a woman as much as I did that witch. Everything I was doing I did for the passion of vengeance.

The bells rang again. With more smoke coming from the incense and shoes tapping on the wooden floor in rhythm with a growling that shook the whole room, she took a seat in the style of a warlord.

"Who are you?" I asked.

"I'm Balagril," said the woman, in the voice of a man.

"Give me the address of my enemies and the traitor," I asked him, referring to those who killed Kenny.

After we planned revenge and paid a bail of eight thousand dollars to get Forty-Seven out of immigration, he returned to work with that group we were after, an act which we considered high treason; it demanded his head. That witch and her friend evoking the spirits of war, flatly denied me the addresses with the excuse that "it was not time to shed blood."

We paid a private detective and in less than twenty-four hours he supplied us with the necessary information.

That same Friday, October 25th of 1985 at night, we celebrated my twenty ninth birthday. Each one of the guys had a date. We were at a nightclub where the popular salsa orchestras played. We sat at a corner table against the wall and, although the girls insisted, we did not go out much to the dance floor. Like a baseball team gathered at the pitcher's mound, we were brainstorming strategies against the opposing team.

Later at a more private place we discussed in detail the information we had received from the private investigator, who proved to be very effective in his spying techniques. Nothing was missing. We had the best weapons. We bought two machine guns, pistols and handguns with ammunition boxes, silencers, bulletproof vests and other accessories. Looking at our artillery, analyzing all the acquired information and thinking about the five people and their companions who would fall victim to our surprise attack on October 31st, Halloween, we thought that New York would remember this event as "The Halloween Massacre".

# Surprise for us

On Sunday, October 27th, that same year, I invited my close friends and family to celebrate an hour of prayers to dedicate the closet altars I had made with my own hands. After the boring repetitions – borrowed from Catholic traditions - the witches began acting up. They were about to take on the personas of different spirits. The first one began jerking, growling, and foot stomping.

"Bellier Bel Cam is here," said Jocy, Lento's wife, bowing in adoration.

"There comes Ogun," Mother announced joyfully while she served drinks in honor of her new apartment.

Once they were "in character," they seated themselves and began predicting futures of the guests, one at a time, while everyone drank glasses of expensive liquor -- Remy Martin, Hennesy, Courvassier, among others. They filled large cups and blew smoke in the faces of those present while communicating their predictions.

"You are a child of the mysteries," said one of the witches in the voice of a tough man.

"They sure don't say anything to me," protested my uncle Bartolo, "because I'm flat broke. You're only here because my nephew has a lot of cash."

"Bartolo, stop drinking,"my mother yelled.

"You don't know anything. You're a pair of frauds," he said, shaking his finger at them. "Witches are nobodies."

Suddenly, the witch in a trance with Bellier Bel Cam, got a knife out and pretended to stab herself in the abdominal section.

"Lies," Uncle Bartolo challenged. "Let me have your knife and you'll see how I cut out your guts." The witch kept stabbing at herself frenetically.

"Who are you trying to fool? You're all fake!," Bartolo yelled over the shoulders of those who tried to stop him from a physical confrontation with the woman.

After calming everyone down, I was temporarily blessed until a new "protector" could arrive from Haiti.

The following day, I knelt down before the altar and read some recitations that had been recommended to me. I specially remember the one about the righteous judge. While prostrate, I felt that someone was walking in the house. I called mother. But no one answered. I went to her room, but she wasn't there. I looked all over the apartment. Everything was calm. So I lay down again. All of a sudden, every time I lay in front of the altar, I felt as if someone ran out of the living room like lightning. I ran to my room, took my gun and checked room by room. I searched the closets, behind the curtains, the refrigerator, the kitchen, etc. Everything was in its place. Even the money suitcase that had twenty thousand dollars in cash was in the exact same place in the closet where I had placed it the day before. However, the atmosphere in the house was very strange, so strange that I preferred to go out for a while.

The following morning, Tuesday, October 29t ,1985, while leaving my house, my mother took me by the arm and said, concerned:

"Son, don't leave the house today. I dreamed the police arrested you; and that when they handcuffed you, you loosed yourself and threw the cuffs in the air.

"That means that even if I do get arrested, I will be free," I said sarcastically, laughing as I said good-bye to her.

That night I went to visit the guys, especially to see Rony to talk to him about something happening in his family. At that time, there was a lot of traffic at the apartment. Clients had multiplied. I spoke with Rony about five minutes.

"Sal, get out of here. The block is hot," said Sweepy.

I walked to the door when someone began knocking at it. When I checked through the peephole and saw that it was one of the workers, I opened the door. Suddenly, the door was pushed violently. I resisted with the help of a wooden bar we had nailed on the floor parallel to the door.

"Police!" We heard a sharp voice yelling. The agent tried to force his short barrel rifle through the narrow opening. I threw myself on the weapon like a wild beast. A second agent managed to put his gun through a three-quarter-inch opening near the top of the door. I tried to give my friends as much time as I could for them to get rid of the cocaine. In the middle of this intense battle and the confusion, a blasting sound was heard. The police and I fell to the floor in a fight. Boots and shoes tromped over me. I thought they had wounded one of the guys. They dragged Sweepy, Rony and I to the living room. They threw us on the carpet. Some of the officers pushed, beat and kicked some of those under arrest, yelling insults at them.

"These cowards hit us because we are cuffed," I protested out loud.

"You're the wrestler that broke the sergeants hand, right?" asked the officer,

kicking me in the thigh at the same time.

"You beat me because you are at an advantage. You know I'd beat the living daylights out of you, man to man," I complained.

He came up to me, took me by the shoulders and made me stand up. A second agent put himself between us and told me not to challenge him.

"None of you is a match for us," said Sweepy. "Let's see who's brave enough to take his badge off and put his little gun away and show how much of a man he is."

Police officers were running all over the apartment. They ran to the living room informing the sergeant of the evidence they had found: cocaine, different types of bullets.

"Harry," one of them called from the bedroom in a loud voice.

Chills ran up and down my spine.

Something was not right. They took us out of the apartment very quickly. We heard them talking about the bomb squad. As soon as we arrived at the 26th precinct, the police officer that Sweepy and I had challenged approached our cell, pointed at me and, with an ironic smile, said: "We have enough evidence to hang you forever. You will have to explain to the court what you were going to do with a bomb."

"Give me a cigarette, Rony," I asked.

"Give me one, too," asked Sweepy, who, just like me, had quit smoking several months ago.

We were questioned separately and pressured to tell who our connection was in exchange for our release. We acted as if we knew nothing. They accused us of hiding things behind a phony wall in the bedroom. They said they had found bullet holes in the wall, mattress and phone book.

I felt a strong weight come on me, pressure in my chest. I couldn't see straight. Would these police officers invent charges? Would the guys sell out to an undercover? Would they find the hiding place containing the remaining kilos? What was all this talk about a bomb? Why had we stored so many explosives in that apartment? Why had I decided to go there after such a long, intentional absence? What had happened? Why did we get arrested? Why did that worker allow himself to be used by the police? Doesn't he know that he will die for his treason?

At that time of the morning, inside the dungeon of the 26th precinct, the cell of my first and last arrest, the guys were sleeping. One was on the bench, and other on the bare floor. I was not able to sleep. I lit a cigarette. I continued to sink into the abyss of my thoughts. I thought for a long time, and reached the conclusion that I would unquestionably be an old man the next time I'd see the streets.

*Two Ways*

# 13
# ENCOUNTERS

The new day didn't seem to offer any hope. Our lawyers gave us the bad news that the prosecutor was rigorously trying to convince the judge not to allow us out on bail, or at least to set it high enough so we couldn't get out.

"The problem here is not drugs, but a bomb and a criminal record," said my lawyer.

"Maybe two of you will be released," said one of the other lawyers.

Threats began exploding against anyone who would say anything out of fear of prison.

"This coward had to let the police scare him into coming and knocking on the door," the guys accused Chichi.

"He'll remember us," we continued blustering against our traitor until they began calling us by name.

There was a lot of movement in the court building. The deputies were going from one place to the other. This worried us. This was not our first time. We knew very well how to discern the atmosphere and the behavior of the guards when a case was unusual. Finally, when they took us out of our cells to face the judge, we were accompanied by a swarm of guards. Usually, only one escorts a prisoner, even two or three prisoners, at a time. But now there were two or three guards for each one of us, especially for Sweepy, Rony and me. In one quick look inside the courtroom, I saw my mother's bloodshot eyes, full of sadness. I saw Teresa, the witch, chanting her spells in our favor. Her face was totally transfigured because of her concentration on the spiritual beings.

Her spells had no effect on the prosecutor who declared us a menace to society, and supporting his claim with the detailed reading of the criminal records for: Salvador Sabino and Ramon Nuñez (Sweepy). The judge set a bail lower than what the prosecutor had recommended, but much higher than the one our lawyers had suggested: two hundred fifty thousand for Sweepy and for me and seventy five thousand for Rony and the other two accused.

Finally, we were escorted to "The Tombs," the detention house for men in Manhattan. The smells, sounds and sights were no longer strange. The behavior of the prisoners was familiar. Some seemed to feel at home. Anything needed for subsistence could be found in their cells: clothes, radios, toiletries etc... These are the ones that adapt to the environment. Others seemed never to adapt. These are the ones that live oppressed, suffocated and desperate. Usually, they go to great lengths to find ways to communicate with the outside world by phone or mail, or any means of communication or escape.

Although almost all prisoners are sad, the ones that suffer most are those who adapt but never surrender to the restricted life of being locked up.

## Too soon to go back

I had learned that adaptation is a necessary process to avoid unnecessary suffering but I wasn't ready to accept being imprisoned again. I decided to fight for my liberty. We heard that the mafia in the well-known case of "The Pizza Connection" employed very good lawyers. Therefore, we decided to hire some of these lawyers as well. They charged forty thousand dollars plus court costs if they became necessary. I personally employed two witches and a "Baca" witchdoctor. This latter one was more expensive than my lawyer. Another witchdoctor offered to become my partner in order to protect my property. I also wanted a piece of the action. I asked a Bronx witch to send a book about spirits.

"If I get a hold of that book, I'll get out of here myself", I thought, "I'm wiser than that witch". I asked my mother to bring me the book the following day.

"Did the witch send the…", I asked my mother in the visiting hall.

Once in my cell, I opened the sack, took the clothes out and some other things she brought. Everything she brought was secondary to me; my freedom was priority. The book was at the bottom of the sack. Finally, I touched it, seized it, and took it out from the sack. What a grief! What disappointment!

"That witch is making fun of me because I'm in prison. I'll teach her a thing or two. Nobody fools me like this. The witch has sent me a Bible!" I vowed to get back at her.

I always believed that the Bible was a holy book. I took it and placed it on my dresser. I decorated it with a glass of water, a banana, and a piece of bread on the side. I opened the Bible to Psalm 23 and placed an apple on top of it, just as the second witch had recommended.

"I am San Carlos Borromeo. Read Psalm 23," she had said, sitting atop the popular creature called Candelo. Teresa, this last witch, did not care. The other witches were after their salary. "Garzahn (Boy), wit two thousand dollar I make dee job. I talk wit you undir dee bed," proposed the Haitian through one of the witch doctors, for he would not talk over the phone,although he did visit my house on payday.

On the other side our lawyer gave us good news. During the ballistic tests, the bomb was declared inoperative. This brought much relief. However, they also said that the police had an informant that was willing to render a statement that would incriminate us to the last detail. Naturally, this was worrisome. I would call the lawyers to suggest different ideas and legal strategies, which I believed would give us the victory in this case. We didn't care about the money we had to invest into this case. Lento couldn't distribute from the same spot where we had been arrested, but I sold the last of things I had: Uzi and Mack 10 machine guns, among other weapons, explosives and special cocaine chemical preparations and paraphernalia. Once in a while, I would call one of my clients and put him in contact with a friend.

One time, I was sitting on the steps smoking a cigarette, while I was waiting to make a phone call. He seemed to be ignoring the fact that others were waiting to make their calls.

"Hey! Come on let go of the phone, man!" I yelled from where I was sitting. He signaled he would not be long. However, he got carried away again in his conversation.

"If you don't get off the phone right now, you know what's going to happen," I threatened in a strong voice.

"I smell trouble between you and that guy," said another one, worried by the way the other prisoner hung up the phone.

"It seems like people are afraid of that group," I replied while approaching the phone that had just been freed.

I sat down again on the steps, ready for any type of confrontation. I had confidence in my fighting abilities. Apart from that, I was in better physical shape than most of them. A professional wrestler called Buitre approached me. He had cried publicly during his phone conversations over being imprisoned for the first time.

"I'm going to tell you something, old prisoner," I said. "You shouldn't cry in front of the rest. They will say that Dominicans are cowards." I knew the others scorned him secretly.

"I cry because of what has happened to me; but if an inmate laughs at me, I'll break his back," he said. Soon enough, he proved his claim by overcoming two inmates at the same time in the gym. Other prisoners joined the conversation.

"Watch out," said one. "They're shooting you some bad looks."

"I wish that phone guy would say something to me," I said in a challenging tone.

"Do you know why you are always frustrated?" asked someone I hadn't seen before.

"Why?" I asked, standing and ready to fight.

"Because you need Jesus Christ," he answered in a resoundingvoice full of both courage and tenderness.

# An encounter that changed my life

These words, those of my friends and, especially, those of my uncle echoed in my ears. Finally, Sweepy and Rony, who were in the unit across from me, yelled asking for cigarettes. I suggested to them that we meet at the law library or in the gym but they told me that the chapel was the only place open at that time. I went there for the cigarettes but I left terrorized because I believed that everything the preacher was saying was referred to me and came against everything I was. At that time, I had begun reading the Bible frequently

"So that's why you haven't been out playing chess or dominoes?" complained a friend who surprised me while I was reading on my bed.

"Be careful, old Salva of being brainwashed, Sal! Don't go mad!" he warned me. His observation was right, in one sense. Usually, a prisoner entertains himself by doing physical exercise and playing games among other things. I was captivated with reading the Bible. This was my recreation. While I read it I felt an incomparable peace.

Slowly, I began changing without noticing it. I limited my games and telephone calls to learn about the drug dealing successes in my neighborhood. I began detesting violence. I told a friend who wanted to marry me that I was no longer interested in her visits. Finally, the "Baca" sent a list of spirit names for me to invoke for help in getting out of prison. Then the "Baca" and the two witches asked that I call them more frequently. However, I had a dream that left me so perplexed that I chose to avoid them. I dreamed that a monster, in the shape of a giant black bear with three heads, one large and two small, was coming cunningly and aggressively to destroy me. I understood that the dream was about the "Baca" and the two witches. Therefore, after confirming with the Bible and with my uncle the pastor that some of those names represented Satan himself, I decided to throw them in the toilet.

Several days later, they invited me to chapel again. Only this time I challenged the Lord, in prayer, saying: "Lord, if you really live as the Bible says, and if you really live as the preachers say, wake me on time to go to chapel. I will go and never again take a step back.

Usually, I fell asleep during the early morning hours. I spent the nights thinking how to avenge myself against people with whom I had problems. But that night was very different. I believe I went to sleep as soon as I finished praying. I went to sleep knowing that the Bible says "for everyone who calls on the name of the Lord will be saved" and "Call to me and I will answer you and tell you great and unsearchable things you do not know" (Romans 10:13; Jeremiah 3:33 NIV).

At about five thirty in the morning, I woke up hearing a voice that didn't belong to any of my fellow inmates: "Salvador." At first I thought I was hearing voices as a result of drug abuse and poor sleep. However, I couldn't deny the fact that I wasn't hearing the voice of a man. It was the indisputable, unassailable voice of the Lord. It was like "the sound of many waters." This voice not only filled my cell with His glory, He touched the deepest part of my inner being. His touch reached a place so deep that dirty money had never reached it. He touched me where drugs never had before. Jesus, the Redeemer was there, Jesus the Savior, the one who saved Matthew and Zacchaeus, men that walked in the wrong way, detestable crooks such as I, rejected by society. I tried to run outside my cell. I ran from one side to the other totally drenched in perspiration. I yelled ,calling the guard. I called other inmates. I couldn't hold myself one more minute on my feet. Hallelujah! The presence of the Lord was irresistible, almost tangible. I felt glory that was so real, I didn't doubt that the Lord was visiting me. I fell on my knees, while confessing: "You are the Lord! You are the Lord! You are the Lord! Therefore God exalted him to the highest place and gave him the name that is above very name, that at the name of Jesus every knee should bow, in heaven and on earth and under the earth, and every tongue confess that Jesus Christ is Lord, to the glory of God the Father" (Philippians 2:9-11 NIV)

# Ultra radical change

As soon as I obtained permission to go to the chapel, I quickly left. The preacher made a call that I understood I should respond to. However, I resisted, staying seated, mostly because there were some guys I knew at the service. I returned to the next service. To my surprise, there were more people at the chapel than I expected. Sweepy and Rony were there, and even worse, a Colombian friend who had lost his four front upper teeth. When I got up from my chair to respond to the altar call the preacher was making, I almost lost heart due to the Dracula-like stare my friend with the missing teeth shot at me.

"What are you doing?" I heard a friend ask.

"Are you going mad? What's wrong with you?," said Sweepy, totally surprised.

"I will walk toward that altar and never turn back," I said inside myself. "I don't care what they say. I will give myself to the Lord wholeheartedly."

When we left the chapel, the guys bombarded me with their comments.

"I imagine you will quit smoking," said Sweepy, to whom I gave the last thirteen boxes of cigarettes I had.

"I'm not doing drugs either," I answered back.

I chose to spend most of my time in the cell. I spent most of the day and the night studying Scripture. One day I was so touched by John the Baptist's and the Lord Jesus' messages that I left the cell with my Bible in my hand and began proclaiming at the top of my voice: "Repent for the Kingdom of Heaven is at hand." The guys that played dominoes and chess, those that watched TV or were simply chatting, were greatly surprised.

"Now, because Salvador Sabino has converted we too are obliged to convert" they said. "but I'm convinced by no one." Although some scoffed and others got angry, the following Sunday twenty of them attended chapel service.

I began having a series of dreams, almost daily. I dreamed that I swam in a crystal clear river that was very refreshing. I looked like a child jumping in the water, spurting water with my hands, arms and feet. I was a swimming fish. I wet my head several times while laughing hilariously. What great joy I felt!

One time, I dreamed I was at the edge of a very wide river. I marveled at the beautiful scenery: the nearby pastures, the gray stones that seemed to be carefully placed in a very orderly way, the many leafy trees. It was a clear morning, with a tropical temperature. All this scenery seemed to caress its most remarkable element: the river. Its current seemed to give life to the countryside.

"Come, board the boat," said a man with a conical velvet hat whose great round wings hindered me from seeing his face.

I boarded the wooden boat surrounded by an impeccable view. The man rowed and rowed the boat without saying a word. I had to stand up because the beauty on the other side of the river was so enticing. The trees were unimaginably beautiful. Everything was very impressive.

"Sir, where are you taking me," I asked curiously.

"To the other side," answered the voice from under the hat.

This dream lingered in my mind and was strangely comforting.

# A Bible school across from my cell

I called my lawyer and said I had decided not to lie to the judge about my guilt.

"Are you crazy? The evidence they have will disappear with the new strategy Robert Leighton and I have," said Morton Kats.

The Leightman firm agreed because they represented Rony, who didn't have a criminal record. At the end, a minimum sentence was negotiated for the three of us: Rony, from one to three years; Sweepy, from six years to life and I, from four and half to nine years plus the remainder of my last sentence, which added up to a total of twelve years.

We were transferred to The Blocks to wait for the results of the negotiation that was taking place concerning our sentence. That place was a zoo compared to the The Tombs. The cells were made out of old iron. In the Tombs, the cells were modern rooms. In the blocks, there were traditional cells that sent you one message: "You're a prisoner."

An inmate interrupted my thoughts.

"Sal, tell the C.O. to bring you over to side B," yelled an acquaintance from the neighborhood. In fact, I was somewhat afraid of The Blocks. There was less control over the activities of the inmates which left a little more freedom. But there was also greater corruption in drugs and violence. Besides that, the number of friends multiplied. I had to be aggressive from the beginning. I couldn't take a step back.

"Did you bring something back from The Tombs," said a friend, referring to some type of drug.

"Yes, I did," I answered while he helped me carry my sack of clothes and books to cell 2B1 of block 4.

"I brought Christ," I said, patting him on the back.

"Don't tell me you've converted," he exclaimed, totally surprised.

"Jesus is the only way. The streets are a big disappointment, my friend," I testified.

That same night, while I walked by other cells greeting some friends, I saw an inmate reading his Bible.

"Are you a Christian?" I asked.

"Yes, I belong to the Lord," answered Ramon Eduardo Bonilla, extending his hand.

We invited other inmates to study the Bible with us. On Good Friday, we celebrated a special service. Twenty-eight inmates responded to our invitation. As we took turns preaching the Seven Words, the guard on duty came in front of the group and took me aside.

"What do you tell them?" he asked.

"We tell them that although we are prisoners, we can be free because Jesus '...came to proclaim freedom for the prisoners.' And 'If the Son sets you free, you will be free indeed." (Luke 4:18; John 8:36 NIV)

Finishing our glorious service, almost every one of the participants confessed Christ as their Lord and Savior. Given my lack of experience I made the inmates with the worst reputations kneel on the hard, cold cement, because I believed they were less worthy of the Lord.

"Kneel there and repent so that the Lord will forgive you and deliver you," I would yell at them, while laying my hands on some of the most dangerous prisoners.

The Bible study was dealing a severe blow to the kingdom of darkness. Many prisoners converted and came to the chapel with us every Sunday. However, not everything was easy. A word went around that an inmate with a very bad reputation who had just arrived on the block planned on initiating a campaign to abuse the peaceful people. Although I taught out of the Book of Job, I made myself a 12-inch steel blade. I taught every afternoon, but without letting go of the blade.

"We Christians don't fight with such weapons,"Bonilla rebuked me.

"Quiet, hypocrite. Didn't David kill Goliath?" I yelled at him in front of eight men that studied with us. "I will not attack anyone but if someone attacks me I will not let him have his way.

"Christians must turn the other cheek," someone said.

"Sabino, give me your weapon. You belong to the Lord. This guy doesn't dare touch you," suggested Manny "el Boricua." He spoke in love. "Give it to me."

I didn't give it up. The next day someone asked me for a cigarette.

I told him I didn't smoke.

"So now you show off your Christianity," he scoffed. I chased him all over the block. Finally he went to seek out the help of Manny and others to make peace with me. I used the opportunity to clearly state that no one was to tempt me because if I backslid that person wouldn't do very well.

I spent several days in a bad mood, looking for a reason to fight, but it seems that God didn't want that for me. A young man of delicate appearance who had recently converted came to me trembling in fear because a veteran prisoner had tried to abuse him while he was taking a shower. This kind of abuse is not as common as they say, but it is real in the prison world. I wanted to solve this problem by my own means. I returned to the old way for a while. I took my blade, ran quickly to the bathroom but found nobody there. When the other prisoners saw me so furious, they said: "The devil is inside Sabino. Christians are supposed to turn the other cheek."

I was indignant over the scoffing that simple Christians frequently suffered. I approached a group of people making jokes. Without any spirituality, I yelled: "I'm willing to do what it takes, and whoever dares to do anything to anyone of these Christians, I'm going to crack his head."

Minutes later in the solitude of my cell I felt a terrible conviction. I had been a violent and vindictive man all of my life but now, although my friends wouldn't see me that way because of the incident, that area of my life was in still in the conversion process. I repented and did away with the weapon.

"Salvador, the block is hot," Gardi Gordi secretly said through an opening in the gate that united side A and B of Block 4.

"Everything is fine now," I answered calmly.

"The problem is that you are not controlling the area," he complained.

"Gardi, I'm no longer into that," I answered. "I belong to Christ."

"Take this blade and take control," he insisted. "Don't chicken out now. The only thing out there is a bunch of idiots."

I rejected this and other temptations until I was sentenced and sent back to the prisons in northern New York State.

# A celestial calling to preach the Word of God

During the process of admission to the new prison system, I asked the Lord not to allow them to transfer me to a far away prison because of my mother and her fragile health. As much as I would ask her not to visit me, she paid no attention. The Lord answered my prayer. They took me to Fishkill Correctional Facility, an hour and a half from the city. As soon as I arrived at Fishkill, I began fasting. My hunger for God drove me to pray, read the Bible and any book that spoke of the kingdom. I meditated day and night on the Lord. I knew I was not alone in my cell. During that fast, something happened that led me to a deeper surrendering to the Lord. I dreamed I was in a building impeccable in construction and design. Apparently, I had just taken a shower. I had sandals and a white robe on; simple but delicate, very different from the green color uniform and black boots I wore in prison.

Everything in that place was different. I knew in the Spirit I was visiting heaven. I was expecting something. Suddenly, when a door opened to my left, a giant hand showed up and spoke more eloquently than any human voice. It was the powerful hand that had sentenced the Babylonian king Belshazzar, writing on the wall: MENE, MENE, TEKEL, PARSIN. Numbered, numbered, weighed, divided. With this sentence the king Belshazzar lost his kingdom and also his life, but I was not Belshazzar. Even though I had walked in his sinful ways, there was a difference. I entered into Christ's presence as a redeemed person. Christ himself had cleansed me with His precious shed blood on the cross of Calvary. He allowed me the entrance to His throne room.

The hand directed me: "Come and enter into my Kingdom". I came out through that door and stood by its side. As I looked sideways, I was able to see the leg of a giant sitting on a throne. I didn't look upon his face out of reverential fear. Suddenly, both of His hands came upon me, dressing me with a very precious garment, never imagined by a human designer. The garment was golden and adorned with all the jewels and precious stones mentioned by the Apostle John in his Revelation vision: diamonds, emeralds, and rubies, among many others.

Brother, be faithful even unto death. The garments that Jesus Christ has for you are much more valuable and precious than the royal garments of earthly kings, princes, and other authorities.

The Lord was enjoying dressing me up. His hands caressed me, they tickled me while they dressed me. Rivers of living water were running on the inside of me. The whole outfit had been fitted to perfection. Everything was my exact measure, as if my size had been taken in advance by a heavenly tailor. Each believer's garment is ready, prepared to his or her exact measure.

There are precious garments for you in heaven!

His hands disappeared upward for a moment and then came back with a solid gold crown such as I had never seen.

When Jesus placed this crown on my head, rivers of living water were running inside and all over me, tears of joy began rolling down my cheeks while I was exalted by an the infilling of an irresistible power. As I was being filled with the power, I was growing and growing rapidly until I reached a gigantic stature.

Suddenly, I looked in front of me and saw a great multitude. There was a great jubilee in heaven, thousands upon thousands of people from every race dressed in many colors jumped out praising the Lord. "Glory to God", they shouted, "blessed is the One who sits on the Throne". The Heavens were shaken by the praise of the Redeemed. They worshipped with all of their strength, and with every type of instrument. No one was silent there. Everybody was jumping and shouting: Hallelujah!

Next, the Lord covered my mouth with His right hand, telling me: "Preach my Word". At that moment I remembered reading in the Bible: "Woe to me if I do not preach the gospel of Jesus Christ! Woe to me if I do not preach! For God so loved the world that he gave his one and only Son, that whoever believes in him even after experiencing the evil path, the way of drugs, religion, shall not perish but have eternal life. Woe to me if I do not preach that Jesus Christ is the way, the truth and the life; the first and the last, the Alpha and Omega, the beginning and the end, He who was, and who is and is to come, the Almighty!

Consequently, I was in the Spirit in such an awesome way. I was surprised by the things the Lord did. Although it was only four months since my encounter with Jesus in the solitude of my prison cell and I had no pastor to teach me, I totally devoted myself to prayer, fasting and reading the Word. My hunger for God and His presence increased every day. Even though I was imprisoned, I was free. I was able to see the things that were happening in the spirit world. Every so often I would awake at midnight and see angels surrounding my bed.

One night, an imposter tried to fake being an angel. And even though he was dressed in luminous clothes, I could see that he really was an evil spirit.

"Leave!" I commanded, "I rebuke you in Jesus' Name!" And he fled from my cubicle.

On another occasion, while I was fasting, I saw angels worshiping and someone sitting on a descending throne. He looked like Jesus but his eyes were red.

"Who are you?" I asked. "Who are you?" He answered by growling twice. "You're not Jesus," I said. "You have the eyes of a marijuana smoker. Since when does Jesus smoke marijuana? You are a demon dressed as an angel of light. I rebuke you!"

I heard a woman in the visit hall tell a dream that caused her much concern "I dreamed that before leaving Puerto Rico, I left a flower vase on my living room table. All the flowers were natural except one. And the artificial one was making the rest wither."

"This dream has a warning from God," I said. "You left someone at your home that is not genetically from your family. This person is causing strife in your home."

Some time later, the lady told me she had to fire her employee because she surprised her by being unfaithful to her. The interpretation of that dream caused this sister's faith to be strengthened in the Lord.

How much my life had changed! I rejoiced in the frequent angelic visits. Sometimes, walking from one place to the other in broad daylight, my eyes were opened suddenly to the spirit world. I could see angels and demons. Reading the Bible with three brothers, one of their faces was transformed suddenly. His beard and eyebrows grew, the skin of his face was drawn in to the bone and horns grew out of his head.

"I cast you out Satan!" I said in a very authoritative way.

The Christians there rebuked me. I asked the brother to forgive me.

That same week it was discovered that he had been casting spells for unbelieving inmates in exchange for cigarettes. He dressed in his bed sheet, wrapped a scarlet turban on his head, placed a cigarette in his mouth and pretended to be a witch doctor.

In this way he tricked them out of their cigarettes, food and other valuables with ridiculous predictions.

Many times I felt my ears become more sensitive to sound and that someone spoke to me through a loudspeaker. Sometimes I felt someone touch me. One night I felt the Lord sit on my bed and hugged me. I hugged Him, too, and kissed Him on the cheek. Right when I was about to say something to Him, He extended His hand and touched my forehead. I fainted and fell asleep on my bed with the same peace I imagine that Ezekiel, Daniel and John felt when they were in the presence of the Lord and could not even remain standing. (Ezekiel 1:28; Daniel 10:9; Revelation 1:17)

I had experienced sensations from different kinds of drugs. And as a man of the street, I had ventured into the pleasures of this life. For them, I risked my existence. I was on the verge of death in hospitals and spent most of my youth behind bars. All this for a short time of pleasure. If drug addicts would know this! If those seeking pleasure in life would just understand that they will never find real satisfaction in that fashion! There is a way that seems right to a man, but in the end it leads to death. (Proverbs 14:12 NIV) Now that I can compare, there is no pleasure that can measure up to the joy one experiences living in a personal relationship with the Lord. The path of life leads upward for the wise to keep him from going down to the grave. (Proverbs 15:24 NIV)

# 14

# COMMISSIONS

Although we didn't have a local pastor to watch over us, volunteers would come to minister to us simply because they wanted to honor the Lord's commission: Remember those in prison as if you were their fellow prisoners (Hebrews 13:3a NIV). There were also mature prisoners that helped us in our walk with the Lord concerning the Scriptures. However, the highlight of all this is that the Holy Spirit was leading us. It wasn't strange to hear a believer in prison say that the Lord had visited him in his cell.

Whoever has my commands and obeys them, he is the one who loves me. He who loves me will be loved by my Father, and I too will love him and show myself to him. (John 14:21 NIV) Most of the prisoners who love the Lord learn during their spiritual childhood that the Lord Jesus is not a historical Christ who died on a cross, in a far away city named Jerusalem about two thousand years ago; but that Christ is real, today, passing through solid cement walls and steel bars to reach that one lost and suffering lamb with his unconditional love.

## The commission to pray for the sick

Early one morning, approximately six months after I came to know the Lord, I was resting and contemplating the heavens through the iron bars of my prison cell. I saw in the sky a great sign. There was a herd of black horses ready to be mounted. Riders appeared and mounted the horses in a hurry. However, no one mounted the white horse that was in the forefront. That horse was bigger than the rest. Suddenly, a tall vigorous man appeared on the scene and sat upon the animal with agility and grace.

"Let's give Sal a message," he said to the rest in a commanding voice. All of a sudden I felt as if a thorn had pierced my right ear. It caused me great pain.

"Sal, rebuke him, that is not Jesus," said the Holy Spirit.

"I rebuke you, Satan," I yelled in a loud voice that was heard throughout heaven.

Satan exploded like an atomic bomb. Immediately, I saw a lightning bolt fall from heaven and then turn into a man. This process took several minutes, until the gigantic figure already known to me was seen in all the heavens. He shoneed in the heavens more than the sun in its splendor. But this light did not hurt my eyes. As soon as I saw the Lord again, praise broke forth from my innermost being: "Hallelujah! Blessed is the one who comes in the name of the Lord!"

As the Lord came closer, I noticed He had a rod in his right hand and with the fingers of His left hand He made the sign of peace. Then the Holy Spirit came upon me. He laid me on the bed just as a mother does with a tender newborn. I am not sure if I was sleeping, I don't believe so, but neither can I affirm being awake. Nevertheless, I believe I saw with my own eyes the pleasant brightness that entered through the iron bars of my window. Once it came close to me, the Lord firmly placed His hand on my shoulder and commissioned me: "Pray for the sick".

The One that said to His disciples: "Heal the sick, raise the dead, cleanse those who have leprosy, drive out demons" (Matthew 10:8 NIV). The Jesus that said: And these signs will accompany those who believe: In my name they will drive out demons; they will speak in new tongues...they will place their hands on sick people, and they will get well." (Mark 16:17-18d NIV) While the Lord placed His hand on my shoulder, I was filled with an indescribable supernatural power. That power flowed through my being burning my body with an all-embracing fire, which began flowing out of my hands in the form of electric discharges. When I felt the Lord was leaving through the door without opening it, I sat on my bed laughing hilariously and uncontrollably because of the powerful joy that embraced me.

"Who was here?" asked Cuba my cell mate, very surprised.

"Jesus of Nazareth," I responded without hesitation.

"Tonight, I'm going to church with you," said this man who had repeatedly rejected all my invitations.

Sometime later we were praying and a guard joined us in prayer.

"Pray for my wife. She's been diagnosed with cancer for the third time," he asked with tears in his eyes. Almost a month later the guard was praising God. His wife was declared healed!

# The Lord empowers to pray and preach

My favorite moments were those I shared with the Lord in my cell. In the chapel it was different. There was a strong group of faith believers at the Fishkill ministry. However, there was much doctrinal diversity. This caused a lot of strife. When the time came for the brother in charge to leave, as it was customary, he had the right to choose the next leader with the handing over of the ecclesiastic files.

"I'm giving the book to the person that God told me would be the next Hispanic pastor," said brother Segundo handing the book over to me.

"Sabino is a child," Willie Gines protested. "You can't do such a thing."

"Brother Segundo, I'm not ready for this position," I replied refusing to accept it.

"If you disobey God because of your poor faith, that's your problem," he said with conviction. "Don't allow yourself to be frightened by the vain wisdom of men because '…God chose the foolish things of the world to shame the wise.'"(1 Corinthians 1:27a NIV)

I resisted until the brother gave up. Then Jose Caraballo was chosen. I learned much from him as well as from Sterling Thompson, who was in charge of the English department and was also my personal teacher.

"You are insatiable," Sterling would say to me because of the many questions I asked him about the Bible. The truth is I had such a hunger for God that I would awake in the early morning hours to pray and study the Word. Every time an altar call for commitment and for the infilling of the Holy Spirit was made I went up front.

One day, Teresa the witch came to visit me and said: "You're still lacking something. You need the baptism of the Holy Spirit". She backslid from the Lord's ways in her youth, but she would soon surrender her life to Him again.

I felt very offended. For a moment I thought something was wrong with me. The truth is I knew I was lacking something. I spent months seeking that baptism. I asked everyone who had received it to pray for me. I anointed myself with oil. Many times I returned to my cell discouraged and unsure of my holiness. But my hunger for Him did not allow me to give up.

"Lord, I hunger for you. I want more of you," I shouted, prayed and even sang to the Lord in the loneliness of my cell.

Well before dawn one morning, I woke up hearing two people talking at one end of my bed. I kept my eyes half opened, nervous and wondering how they had gotten into my cell. I worried that they might jump on me and attack me. I tried to hear what they were saying.

"Let's get closer to him and give him power," I heard one of the visitors say. When I realized they were talking about me, I opened my eyes but a luminous hand covered them immediately and I could see nothing. I felt the hand envelope my face and felt lips touch my left ear. I heard a voice say: "Receive power to pray and preach". Instantly I exploded in tongues and broke the night silence in the unit. Immediately, I heard the sound of the guard's keys as he patrolled, trying to find the source of the strange sound. With enormous effort, I was able to quiet myself. Quickly, I covered myself with the bed sheets and pretended to be asleep.

"Mr. Sabino, what sound was that coming from your cell?," asked the guard. I had to feign sleep. If the guard had learned that the strange sound was coming from my mouth, he would certainly have sent me to the psychiatric ward, as occurred with brother Zenon Collado who was caught speaking in tongues in the solitude of his cell. Undoubtedly, I didn't want to fulfill the Scripture in me that says: "The man without the Spirit does not accept the things that come from the Spirit of God, for they are foolishness to him, and he cannot understand them, because they are spiritually discerned." (1 Corinthians 2:14 NIV)

"Mr. Sabino, are you alright?," asked the guard returning not convinced of my silence.

"Of course I am! I'm doing very well officer," I answered hiding my face from the light of his flashlight.

The next day I felt very happy. Rivers of living water were flowing through me. My joy was such that even my green uniform and black boots seemed to me like the latest fashion. Breakfast tasted delicious. "Your eyes are gleaming," some said.

"That's good stuff," said others, thinking I had smoked marijuana.

On my way to the infirmary, I saw a boxer friend who was holding on to his jaw. He signaled to me that he was in a lot of pain. I looked and it was swollen. As I was walking by him, the Spirit said, "Touch him." Before I could begin thinking about what I was hearing, my hands were on him. "I declare you healed in the name of Jesus". The man began to jump and yell: "I'm healed, I'm healed".

# Commissioned to make a call to the Church

I dreamed that I was flying over the clouds dressed in white, when I heard someone crying. I could clearly see the zinc rooftops like the ones on the homes in San Pedro de Macoris. At a distance I saw a young lady crying bitterly. I saw her only from the back, which was covered by her long hair. I sensed she was very pretty. The thin young woman was moaning pathetically in a loud voice that was heard throughout the heavens. She cried and cried, but I didn't understand the reason for her weeping. I was touched by her attitude and I decided to approach her, at least, to alleviate her grief. Suddenly, a gigantic person appeared at the door. It was the Lord. He was dressed in a brilliant white garment, as always, with His white hair and beard like wool, His face was brilliant as the sunrise. The Lord opened His mouth and pointed at the young lady who had made a pond with her tears. He commanded me to tell her: "Here I am! I stand at the door and knock. If anyone hears my voice and opens the door, I will come in and eat with him, and he with me." (Revelation 3:20 NIV).

Months later, the Lord blessed us with Ernest L. Boston, a new senior chaplain. More than a pastor, this man and his beloved wife Mary, became parents to all of us, especially to me.

"God has called you," said Reverend Boston. "You will preach on Monday, August 17th.

"Today is August 1st," I replied. "Give me more time."

"Those who are called of God should not avoid their responsibility," he said to me.

"What will I preach about?," I asked with some uncertainty.

"If God has called you, he has already given you the message," he affirmed.

"He hasn't given me a message," I said.

"Then I don't know who called you," he said, gazing steadily at me.

Coming out of his office, I turned around and asked him to interpret my dream of the young lady that cried in heaven. As soon as I told him about it, he told me that was the message God wanted me to preach: The young lady represented the Church and her cry speaks of her condition. That Monday, August 17th of 1987, I preached my first message: Jesus is calling you. Two souls came to the Lord. And although I was inexperienced and committed many errors, many of those there were motivated to work for the Lord.

Brothers Hector Anderson, Rafael Nuñez, Paul

Langley, Ed Wicks, Raymond Quiara, Angel Sánchez, Juan Rubio, among many others, were used in that work. Also the ministers and ministries that would bring the Word of God from the outside greatly strengthened us. Our prison congregation entered into a vibrant revival.

# We ministered in the power of the Spirit

It wasn't strange to receive invitations for long periods of fasting, even weeks. There was a spirit of prayer in the ministry, "Raising the Dead," founded by Reverend Boston. He named me assistant to Sterling Thompson in leading the services for the English ministry. Then, brother Jose Caraballo turned over the leading of the Latino services to me.

With the ministry "Raising the Dead" we obtained permission to minister in areas in which we were not allowed to work before.

Of course this doesn't mean we didn't have our share of opposition.

We entered the unit where very few people wanted to go: the AIDS unit. There we got to know a man whose head was very swollen; his body, in contrast, seemed reduced to the size of a child's. Another man had lost his mind and would walk from one side of the hallway to the other cursing a certain ethnic group and swearing to exterminate it.

"Sabino, is that you?", Barbero asked, "I can hear you, but I can't see you". He had gone blind since very young due to his infection. We didn't care what condition they were in, we ministered to those people in love. We prayed for all of them, one by one. They praised God with us in choruses of faith and joy: "Spring up, oh well, within my soul, spring up oh well and make me who-o-ole, spring up, oh well, and give to me, that life abundantly."

"Who gave you permission to be here?," the lieutenant who had just entered the unit yelled. "Return immediately to your unit. You are out of your place!

# Fear of AIDS

A great part of the prisoners were fearful of being infected with the AIDS virus due to their promiscuous lifestyle, and the needles used in applying tattoos and injecting intravenous drugs. I myself worried throughout several nights thinking of the careless relationships I had had with some of the young women from our neighborhood. But during a night vision, I saw myself on a bed and a man dressed as a doctor with a form in his hand approached me and said in a voice of authority: "Ten times you've had contact with AIDS. Ten times I have delivered you." I believed and a test given to me in prison as a prerequisite for family visits was negative.

Five of the church leaders died of AIDS. On one occasion, I was praying with Agustin Masa, my son in the faith and partner in prayer and fasting. We ate and played together. Wherever I went, there he was with me. People compared our relationship to the one between Paul and Timothy.

While we prayed in the second day of a three-day fast, I said to him: "Masa, the Lord is revealing to me that you need to take an AIDS test."

He complied. Two weeks later we wept together.

"The Lord has saved me. I'm ready to go home with Him," he declared with conviction. Sometime after my release, although the police officer at the door of his room initially denied my entrance, Masa recognized my voice.

"Let him come in; he's my father, and has come to say goodbye," he said in a weak voice as he stretched a feeble hand toward me from his hospital bed. The police officer could not hold me back after such a request. He nodded his head and I entered. I hugged him and held on to him while I prayed. I said goodbye to him with a kiss. We agreed to meet in heaven.

Although many died from AIDS, some were delivered from it by the power of God. One night, we convinced a closet homosexual who professed to be an enemy of the cross that he needed prayer.

"I dreamed that you came to my cell sweating and frightened because you had gone to the hospital and they told you that you were infected with AIDS," I told him as soon as he came into my cell. Shock registered on his face.

"The Lord told me that if you don't repent of your wrong ways and of the perversity you secretly practice, very soon this dream will come true," I added. He left enraged. I forgot for a moment we were Christians. I ran out of my cell to find two metal locks and put them in a sock.

"If he attacks me, I'll break his head," I thought, practicing a technique for knocking him down in one blow. He came back to my room with his boots on, a sign he was ready to fight. He asked to come in, sat peaceably on my bed and asked us to pray for him. We anointed him with oil. We prayed in faith while he twisted and turned, until he was delivered.

The next morning he said to me, in the tone a child uses when he receives a new toy: "Last night I dreamed I was drowning in high seas and I desperately tried to save my life. I tried every swimming stroke I knew. I floated in a life preserver, waiting for ships, boats and canoes, but it was useless. I continued drowning. When I believed I was breathing for the last time and had given up, a huge helicopter appeared.. I thought they would throw me a rope. However, a giant man appeared, dressed in white, and said to me in a loud voice that filled the skies: "I am the lifesaver. I am the Savior."

The writer of Proverbs makes no mistake when he says that the way of life is upward. The lifesaver Jesus Christ saves and delivers anyone who is drowning in the waters of this life. Christ also died for drunkards, liars, religious men and homosexuals. So we prayed that the Lord would give him a wife, and in less than a year, we celebrated a precious wedding in the chapel.

# Casting out demons

One day we were walking the hallways from one building to another, when an inmate of over sixty years approached us asking for a match. I wanted to take offense because his question was an insult to my new holy image in the prison. But the compassion of Christ took over.

"Give me a match," the thin and weakened old man demanded

"The match you are asking for only lights your cigarette. You need a match that will light your life. Receive the light of the world, receive the Christ that can light your life," I preached with much fervor.

"I know more about the Bible than you," he said, smiling sarcastically. "I used to preach in the streets."

"Jesus still loves you," I said, approaching him and pushing him toward the stairway of an intermediate building so as to not be seen by the guard. Praying in this way was prohibited.

"Spirit of the devil, I command you to come out of him in the name of Jesus," I yelled while laying my right hand on his forehead.

Instantly, he began to growl, make other sounds and twist in a very strange manner. Two brothers that were with me joined me in the deliverance session. By the work of the Lord the man began to laugh and leap for joy. Finally, he asked, "Where is the Church?" But we couldn't answer him. We had to continue on our way because a guard was approaching us. However, that night we rejoiced when we saw him dancing in our worship service.

Such outward signs encouraged us and confirmed that the kingdom of heaven was real. We knew that although we had lived in wrong ways, that we were caught in the judicial system, that we were isolated and maybe forgotten, the Lord had forgiven us and above all, our names were written in the book of life. "…Her ways are pleasant ways, and all her paths are peace." (Proverbs 3:17 NIV)

# Preparing for my departure

I began receiving messages through dreams and visions from some of the brothers. "You are getting out of prison this year" a visiting minister prophesied. Another one said: "Wait for the faithful wife I will give you." If you have contact with another woman apart from her, you will die of AIDS". And a brother from prison said: "Do you believe you've seen my glory in this place?" Be faithful and you will see much more of my glory wherever you go".

Finally, I dreamed that I took hold of an old official from state parole board, who had the authority to release me.

"Am I leaving or not?" I asked insistently. "Yes or no."

"Let me go. You're leaving!" he yelled, trying to free himself.

The Lord began showing me the mission He would have for me when I was released. Although I was facing deportation charges, I knew that my prime directive, for the time being, was New York City.

# The vision of two principalities

On the sixth day of a seven-day fast, the Lord took me out of the jail in the Spirit. I flew through space. While ascending to the sky, I saw smoke and contamination all over the city. After going around the city, I descended on Columbus Circle, at the New York Coliseum sidewalk, which is 59th Street and 7th Avenue, in the heart of Manhattan. I looked toward the entrance of Central Park. There I saw in the middle of a multitude of youths coming out of the train station, two demons who were taller than a six-story building. They were sitting on great thrones in the middle of a small park located just before the entrance to Central Park. They were twins, and they looked like green-ish frogs with slimy skin. Their aspect was so disgusting that it gave me terrible nausea. Doubling over, I saw these two demonic agents drawing many of these young people toward them as if with an invisible magnet. When they had them in their sphere of influence, they overcame them and bit into their heads with fangs. A healthy young man who allowed himself to be seduced and bitten, would immediate-ly lose half his weight and become a Zombie, just like in the horror movies.

The first of the two demons I saw represented AIDS, which is attacking our youth. The fangs represent intra-venous drugs and illicit sex, the two major ways the disease is transmitted. On the other hand, the ugliness of the demon and the severe weight loss of its victim was a picture of the physical decomposition of those infected by the diabolical and deadly virus.

The second demon was the same in appearance and purpose as the first one. It represented crack cocaine. The fangs here represent the glass pipe, often used in consuming the drug. This demon absorbs the mind, just as the AIDS demon leaves the youth physically deteriorated. The big thrones from the which they operate are a center for inducing all sorts of perversions into big cities like New York, which have allowed free and open operation of the demons of AIDS and crack cocaine.

Doubled over, I spoke to the throngs of young people, but they ignored my words. While I prophesied to them, the two demons saw me. They took their thrones and fled the place.

In a loud voice I said: "By the power of Christ, right now, I command every foul spirit of drugs, AIDS, violence, witchcraft and immorality to leave this place, in the Name of Jesus! Go!"

I remembered that in my days of smoking processed cocaine — free basing —, I wouldn't hear anyone either. I lived in such a state of paranoia that I sometimes believed that anyone approaching me had the intent of attacking me. In this state, I would jump out of windows, thinking that an imaginary enemy or police officer was forcing in the door. I ran the streets of New York, fleeing hallucinations. I cared very little about the difference between good and evil, high and low, sweet and bitter. And I wasn't the only one. I hung out with a gang of vicious demon possessed people just like me — young people, like some today, who perpetrate vile acts of barbarism just to get a dose of drugs to alleviate their cravings.

I risked my life assaulting, kidnapping, wounding people with guns and other weapons. On several occasions I suffered bullet wounds. I saw my friends and girlfriends whom I loved with all of my heart fall lifeless on the streets of Washington Heights, in Manhattan, New York.

All this happened through being involved with drugs:

heroin and especially, base and crack. Thank God for His mercy. Thanks to Jesus for delivering me. The only crack I seek today, the only crack I'm waiting for, is for the heavens to be "cracked," yes, cracked open from one end to the other, that my eyes might behold the Son of Man descending on the clouds with great power and glory.

# The main task: Souls

The Lord showed me several things in preparation for my release. He charged me with several important issues: evangelizing souls was number one on the list of my commissions. The prison ministry was one of the top items on the list.

To everyone we came in contact with, we preached the Word of God. Whoever it was, if not yet a believer, we presented the message of salvation through Jesus. If they were already believers, we would encourage them to be faithful to the Lord. Everyday we would win new prisoners for the Lord, and those who already were living for God we would integrate them in the ministry. We won police officers, volunteers and social workers, generally.

The Christian band "Christ's Messengers" participated in a secular concert contrary to the will of some that believed that our participation in such an event would be an abomination. We ministered to more than five hundred prisoners in the courtyard. Twenty-three of them received the Lord and many integrated themselves into the church. From the day of the concert on, the church began to grow every Saturday.

Finally, the day of my last worship service arrived. We thanked the Lord together. We had worked hard. We honored Him and He rewarded us: the chapel was completely full.

"Attention please! New passes for the chapel will no longer be issued", announced the administration through the loudspeakers. The brothers from the visiting ministries had allowed me to say good-bye preaching the Word of God. They were very happy for my release. But my co-laborers could not completely hide the sadness they also felt. We knew each other so well that I could see behind their smiles. And there was no doubt they knew how I felt: joyful because I was leaving prison, but sad because I was leaving them.

"Sabino, watch out for street temptations. Don't fall," they admonished me with deep brotherly love. If people only knew that those behind the prison bars have a heart! We had spent four years together. We had rejoiced and suffered, and gone through trials together. We were brothers in joy and pain. It was so precious to see how they would come from every unit to worship their God together! I will never forget that day, although we had mixed feelings of sadness and joy, the latter one prevailed because we were saved. Our names were written in the Book of Life.

That day the Word of God sounded like thunder, and praises exploded everywhere. To this day those images live inside of me. How they raised holy hands and shouted praises to the merciful Creator who had delivered them! As I walked away, I could hear in the distance, the precious melody of the choir:

*Libre, tu me hiciste libre*
*Tu me hisciste libre, libre Señor*
*Rotas fueron las cadenzas*
*Que estaban atando mi corazón.*
*¡Libre!*

# 15
## SOULS

What freshness! What a relief! I left the immigration building on Varick Street and walked on the streets of downtown Manhattan for the first time in four and a half years. What a difference between the city and the mountains where I had spent the last four years! What a huge contrast between the chirping of the birds and the peculiar mountain sounds and those of the moving vehicles, horns, ambulance sirens, police cars and fire trucks!

It had been such a long time since I last bought tokens, put them in the turnstile and ran to board the train before the doors closed on my nose. Before this, I would have complained like any other typical New Yorker. One passenger pushed me into another who absolutely refused to budge. One was Chinese, another American; one African, another Latino; one was white, another black or "mulatto."

One laughed while the other yelled and complained. One was big, the other small; one fat, another thin. One was alert, another groggy. One talked, while another read. The D train was full of diversity. It was typical New York rush hour congestion. To me, this natural competition, the pushing and shoving in rhythm with the clacking and screeching of the trains and the slap of footsteps on the platforms and the clicking of the turnstiles at the entrance trumpeted one thing: You are a free man! Free! Free!

This was my third prison exit. The two times before, I had asked a friend to get me a gun, a woman, and some money and drugs, but not this time. Although I feared my own weaknesses in the face of the many temptations that no doubt awaited me, I was a new man. I took my Bible, which was now my gun. I opened my mouth and began to preach on the train.

"Jesus Christ is the Savior for the World," I declared in a loud voice. "He is the true way." I had no doubt that the hand of God was upon my life. He delivered me from serving a greater sentence, which I deserved, because He had a plan for me in the city that I loved so much.

"Many will be won to the Lord," I thought, "God will do great things in this time. I will see New York more full of God's Word than drugs and crime."

## Resist fear

"What is a winner?," an experienced preacher challenged his audience. "A winner is a loser that never gives up. There is no triumph without risk nor victory without struggle!"

"I'm a loser for the third time" a prisoner lamented pessimistically, on the day he was sent to prison a third time.

The options were before me. I was now free to choose between two ways: Go back to my street life or follow the way of Christ. After all, I no longer had someone watching my steps as I had had while in prison. I had more than enough drug connections. I'd always been a go-getter. But I was very sure that my only option was to follow Christ. He would make me a winner!

This world doesn't forgive easily and I was in for a surprise. I thought that with all of my qualifications, I could get a job right away. I had completed an associates degree in humanities, with honors, through Dutchess County Community College. I had served as a counselor to addicts for three years. I thought, that at least, I could get a job in that area.

"You meet all the requirements for this job. However, I'm sorry to say, the hiring guidelines of our institution do not allow us to employ anyone with your criminal record."

I received this reply many times after having passed all the required tests with high scores. The doors were literally closing in my face. I was frustrated in spite of all the hours I spent in prayer. Sometimes I prayed eight and nine hours, face down on the floor, for fasting three or seven days very frequently: "The enemy will not overcome. The Lord will open a door." I couldn't give up.

One day, early in the morning, I was fervently praying for a proposition that I had been given by a good friend. He wanted me to be his partner. Every time he presented the offer, I felt uncomfortable. He was willing to pay me eight hundred dollars a week. But God had another plan.

"God doesn't want you working for a secular company. He prefers that you trust Him," said my pastor, Pablo Fernandez, speaking from God. So I decided to obey the Word of God through my pastor.

On the other hand, my mother would constantly say: "I fear for you, my son, very much." I too feared, however, courage is not the absence of fear, but the ability to resist it. I had made the decision to face fear with all of my strength and with the help of God. I knew my mother very well. My past lifestyle had turned her into a pessimist.

"Don't be childish, Juanita! Open your eyes. Are you

going to let Salvador Antonio break your heart?," my grandmother yelled at my mother between great puffs of smoke. "Even if he is my oldest grandson, if I need to whack him in the head, I'll do it, and that's it!" My grandmother was decisive and aggressive. My mother was passive and even insecure.

Although she was very happy to welcome home her only son, with whom she had struggled all her life, her countenance changed from great joy to extreme anxiety. My mother was still young, about fifty-four years old, but she had lived a hard life. She was the granddaughter of Don Guillermo Jimenez, a skillful businessman, landowner and possessor of a good fortune as they say, daughter of Abigail Jimenez, the oldest son of Don Guillermo. Her father, shortly after she was born, lost his fortune mysteriously, suffered an automobile accident, and went insane.

My mother worked as a maid making a salary of four pesos a month. She had to hand wash clothes and iron large quantities of clothing with a coal-heated iron. She married Delfin Manzueta, a humble and hard working man who fell into the abyss of alcoholism. When, years later, he was reha- bilitated, perhaps because his relationship of twenty-five years had deteriorated so badly, he replaced my mother with a younger woman who received the undeserved trophy of a house, a bank account and retirement to her hometown with her sweetheart.

My mother's only son, Salvador Sabino, stabbed her with the knife of disillusionment. Because of my evil ways, my family, especially my mother, suffered terrible disap- pointment. She reached the point of such hopelessness that when she cuddled me in her arms, she caressed me, dream- ing that I would become a famous doctor, engineer or hon- orable citizen. Who would have said the cuddled mama's boy would become a vile enemy of right, honor and justice? How sad! My mother wept when her irritated relatives, friends and neighbors seemed to blame her for my downfall with subtle reproaches: "I saw your son on drugs" and "I saw your son hanging around with a gang of undesirable criminals."

Praise God! How I rejoiced when I heard that they said to her: "I saw your son proclaiming the Gospel of Jesus Christ" or "I saw your son preaching that Jesus saves, heals, and delivers"!

# A new church in the Bronx

Although I received invitations to preach in different churches each week, my passion was to preach mainly to the lost in my own building, where I won many of my neighbors.

During the summer of 1990 I was invited to a home in Staten Island where a father needed a word of encouragement, for his daughter was ill.

"Thus saith the Lord," said the man, standing up as soon as I finished the message, "the Lord will give you a wonderful congregation, a building full of souls in New York. He is also calling you to minister in Radio Vision Cristiana." The man's name was Cadin Castelo, one of the founders of the radio ministry.

Some time later, when I finished substituting for Pastor Pablo Fernandez on his program of family teaching, came a confirmation: "I see the hand of the Lord upon you. Preach about the grace of the Lord. He will deliver to you many souls that are hurting. He will fill your building with hurting souls," prophesied Brother David Greco, the executive director of the radio.

I also delighted in preaching Christ in the streets of the Bronx. It was an afternoon in May of 1990. The skies were clear, announcing the arrival of summer. People crossed from one side of the street to the other. Some were buying and others just looking at the clothes through the store windows. Most of the people passed by Fordham Road Avenue maybe heading home after getting off the train, the bus, or some taxi. We would take advantage of the time and preach about Jesus, the Son of God.

"Take this free tract," said one of us, while another was preached over a small loudspeaker. Others would approach people and speak to them one-on-one. "He has not come to condemn you; He came to save you." Under rain, sun or snow, we gave testimony of Christ publicly and in the homes.

"In God we will do wonders," Pastor Luis Fernandez preached at the Martinez's home. We had been meeting in homes but we knew it was time to begin gathering in a place where we could all worship God together. As many things of the Lord go, the direction to the building was shown to me in a dream. I dreamt that I was traveling on the No. 4 train. "The building is one stop away," I heard a voice say while I slept.

We had been searching for a place of worship for several months. So I obeyed the voice of God. Since I lived close to Kingsbridge Road, I set out to find a building between there and Fordham Road which is the next train stop when heading south. God had pointed out the place. A small group came out of the Martinez's home on Walton Avenue. We arrived at the Creston Avenue Baptist Church across from Fordham Road, where we began preaching Christ. Who knows the mysteries of God?

That night was glorious in many ways. Pastor Pablo Fernandez brought forth a powerful message. One of the first people to receive Jesus was Francisco Peralta, who would later become one of our pastors. I rejoiced for this and much more. In the crowd that night was the young lady whom I had dreamed would be my wife.

## The enemy never rests

"Don't go to where you've been," prophesied a sister, shaking me by both arms as soon as I got down from the pulpit of the church where my Uncle Antonio pastored. I listened to the voice of God. I decided not to visit my old friends from the neighborhood. "The enemy will not rest" others would say to me. "We need to collect more funds." We need to buy our own building," I would encourage the congregation during most of our activities. "Remember you're in the Bronx. These people live from the welfare system. Look for a small place," some religious leaders advised.

The congregation worked as a unit to collect some seventy thousand dollars in a short time. Some gave five dollars a week and others ten, but some gave all they had.

"This is my tithe of several weeks and this is my offering for the building," said brother Obdulio el Boricua from his bed, extending his hand with a package of envelopes some days before he went on to be with the Lord.

The faithfulness and generosity of these people along with the help of our sister churches pastored by generous leaders likr Pablo and Bernarda Fernandez, and Jose and Millie Felix, who helped us as Hur and Aaron did when they supported Moses' arms. On December 4th 1993, we marched under a baptismal rainfall, via Grand Councourse, until we arrived at 2868 Jerome Avenue. Finally, having

jumped numerous hurdles, we entered our own building --
a supermarket turned into a sanctuary. But we were not
going to settle in without opposition.

"Pastor Sabino, don't ask me about what I'm going to
tell you. Someone's life could be at risk if you react," someone confided to me. "They want you dead. They are willing
to pay any price. They hired an assassin who visited your
church one Sunday with the purpose of shooting you dead
at the right time. God changed plans. Without you realizing it, you greeted that person very warmly. This person
was deeply touched. After he left your church, he came to
my office. He confessed Christ, and shared this experience
with me, asking for absolute secrecy, because he feared for
his life and that of his family. He asked me to tell you to be
careful. Someone is looking to assassinate you in vengeance
for a previous incident." Goose bumps ran all over my body
while this person was talking to me.

It wasn't the first threat I had received from someone
in regards to my past. I didn't remember the incident, not
even vaguely. Four months after leaving prison, my mother
was preparing breakfast for my cousin Richard and I. He
lived with us and ended up as the church pianist. I had
received a vision that an attack was coming.

"Watch yourself Sabino. I've had strange dreams about
you," advised Aurora Martinez – Mara – who, along with
all of her family, supported me. In spite of the warnings, I
was caught by surprise.

"Salvador, someone is calling at the door," my mother
said from the kitchen.
"Who is it?," I asked, seeing a woman who seemed
familiar.
"It's me, Salvador," she responded like an old friend.

"God bless you. Come in please," I said cordially to the young lady and the man who was with her, thinking about what strategy I would use to present Christ.

"We've come to kill you, traitor," they yelled. The man — tall, dark, about two hundred pounds, apparently drunk and sleep deprived — took his gun out.

"Nooo!," yelled my mother from the kitchen, while I jumped on him, knocking him to the ground.

"Let him go," yelled a masculine voice from behind, pressuring my neck with a cold object while he grabbed me firmly by the head.

"If you say a word, I'll kill you," threatened the antagonist, while pointing at my face with a banged up .38 caliber.

"The angel of the Lord encampeth round about them that fear him, and delivereth them," I responded, quoting Psalm 34:7.

"O, so now you're a pastor," the young fair-skinned woman dressed for life on the street mocked me. "You're going to pay me for the four years I spent in prison because of you. You used me!

"I never did business such a lowlife as you," I answered, clenching my teeth.

"Please, my son," said my mother, suffering great pain.

"Shut up, old woman," said the second aggressor who had hold of Richard.

"It would be better if you took what you want. But my mother has nothing to do with my life," I said, very angry by now.

"We're going to spare your life, but we want all the money you have in the house," said the first assailant.

I knew this kind of robber. They weren't killers. Their main interest was getting high. We gave them all the money we had on hand.

"Nobody does that to you and gets away with it. I'm going over there. I'll take a nine-millimeter so they don't mess with you," my friend Charlie said over the phone.

Truthfully, at that moment I wished I had a gun like the nine-millimeter I was offered. I got a tip about who had robbed me.

What a temptation! I had avenged myself all my life. "Anyone who loses their temper would shoot them," I thought in my weakest moments.

On one occasion, I returned to 163rd Street to organize a flea market because a pastor wanted to help me out with a contribution to buy building materials to continue the renovation of our building. One of the guys from the block whose appearance was that of a rat leaving the garbage dump, recognized me: "Is it true you're a pastor now, after such a long street life?" he asked, then fled without giving me time to present Christ to him.

I discerned that I had violated God's command of not returning to the neighborhood. Some minutes later, without my noticing it, someone was trying to shoot me dead from a strategic position in vengeance for a past tragedy. I took my wife and hurried to leave the place.

"There is a woman who wishes you the worst. She has money and is willing to pay whatever it takes to see you dead," another hired killer confessed to me on the phone from a jail in New York. "She says you deserve death, just like her brother got. She wants revenge at any price."

I was a very close friend of the man he was talking about.

"I'm telling you this because I believe you have truly changed. I heard you preaching on Radio Vision Cristiana. You sound good," he said proudly.

I told a pastor friend about the attacks and threats. He said I was not being cautious enough. He sent a homicide detective who was a member of his church to see me. I refused to give him any information. I began receiving constant visits from detectives and then high-ranking investigators at my office.

"You need to take care of your wife and daughter. Do it for them," they urged me with much concern. "You know these assassination attempts are coming from dangerous people.

When I resisted, they suggested some security measures, including training capable men from the congregation to do surveillance during every activity. I complied this thinking these precautions would serve us well in the future as well as the present.

The enemy wouldn't give up. "Don't blame him," said a friend, bursting into laughter. "He's lost one of his best soldiers. Ha, ha, ha!"

During that time my mother had to move to a new address. She had been traumatized by a violent encounter in which she and a friend were held for several hours by six armed men looking for my friend Benny.

"Friend, come over to your old lady's house. I gave the stick to three big ones," Benny had said in code, referring to a robbery of over three hundred thousand dollars. "Tell me, what do I do with this?" I asked him to quickly leave my mother's house.

"Do you want me to leave your part with you?"

I told him to take everything with him. Four hours later, my mother was going to church when gunmen showed up everywhere.

"Where is the money?" asked the fattest one, according to my mother, while he tightened the rope he had around her neck.

My mother left alive, but never again stepped inside that apartment.

Some weeks later my friend "Matt" told me, before he was shot to death, that during a raid someone had killed the fat guy who tortured my mother. My dear friend Benny got on a plane and kept on the run to several different places until he was finally imprisoned again.

"I know the Lord will touch me someday like He did with you," he would say whenever he called me.

It's not good for man to be alone. So I prayed to the Lord not to allow me even to kiss a woman but to draw me close to the one He had chosen for me. "I'm praying to God for the wife He has for you," my pastor friend Guillermo would repeatedly say over the phone. I prayed to the Lord that He would give me a wife that had the street experience, if it was His divine will. The Lord said: "It's not good for man to be alone, I will make him a help meet (Genesis 2:20)

It seems that before God gives a wife to a man, he makes him go to sleep. In a dream, I was at the altar dressed as a bridegroom. "I declare you husband and wife in the name of the…" "But who is the bride?" I asked, interrupting the minister performing the ceremony. Suddenly, ascending over the assembled congregation, was the bride: Kenia Mañana, a very beautiful young lady committed to the Lord.

Just like in a cartoon, I saw my heart leap out of my chest and unite with hers. The two melted together to make one heart, with the taste of caramel apples. Then another dream and our relationship began.

Someone tried to stop it, calling Kenia's spiritual mother and telling her:
"Are you going to allow that young lady to marry an ex-convict?"
It didn't bother me that the sister had an opinion. My reaction was corrective, but in love: "Tell sister so and so to learn that in Christ there is no former or ex anything but new creatures."

Finally, we celebrated a beautiful wedding with a full house, trumpets sounding, confirming my dream. There were many gifts and God's blessing with a wonderful honeymoon in Hawaii. Later came our two beautiful children, Raquel and Gabriel.

## The Lord blesses!

Many of my friends were deported. However, the Lord delivered me. Others came out of prison apparently filled with the Holy Spirit, but then sank again into addiction. I decided to follow the example of the men of God that had a similar past as I but that were now doing something great for the Lord. Of all these, Kittim Silva was a highlight. He was a writer, preacher and recognized Christian leader.

Also, the ministries that visited the Fishkill prison greatly encouraged me to remain faithful to the Lord in my re-entry into society.

"It is difficult to believe your criminal record, however, this court acknowledges your moral rebirth; therefore, it extends pardon number 212c, today...", declared the Hon. Robert Wisel, judge of the Federal Department of Immigration and Naturalization.

"The Lord is good!" my mother repeated over and over, crying for joy and hugging my wife and the defending attorney Maria Liz, who received Christ in our church together with her husband Frank. Both became faithful contributors to the kingdom. Reverend Boston was also there along with my supervising pastor, Pablo Fernandez, celebrating the great victory.

"God has blessed you in everything. The only thing missing now is the granddaughter. I want her to be a girl. If God gives me this, I will die in peace", my mother said.
I disdained the mention of death.

Several months later, she said again: "God has blessed you," as she carried her granddaughter Raquel. "Now I can die in peace." I never imagined her death was so near.

"Salvador, run home", my brother, Miguel Sabino, said over the phone. He was visiting us during professional baseball's off-season. I left the local board meeting, with the board members running after me. The ambulance was across from the building where my mother lived.
Why two police cars? Suddenly, everything went dark. I felt a great burden. I couldn't believe my mother had died. "Not yet, Lord God, please," I pled.

That same afternoon she had prepared a meal for me. We were happy. I went in through the open door.

"What happened? —I asked.
"Calm down, Sabino," begged my brother Hector Anderson who did time with me at Fishkill Correctional Facility and was now also pasturing.

I let out a loud exclamation, reacting in panic and shock. Many hands took hold of me. They belonged to my church leaders, and my wife and other sisters.

My entire world changed. I suddenly felt as if I were moving in slow motion. Time was frozen in the deep pain I felt. What a hard hit! On the living room's floor laid my mother's still body. The woman that had struggled her entire life; who sacrificed everything for me; the one who chose to eat a little plantain and butter so she could save up a hundred dollars to bring me a package of food in prison; the one who in times of need, had always kept calm and found ways to spare me shame.

I laid myself on her and began to cry uncontrollably. Then, my brothers, weeping with me, helped me to place her on the sofa. At only 58, she had had a violent heart attack.
Thank God He had given me the privilege of winning my mother to Christ in one of her prison visits. I was somewhat consoled by testimonies the brothers shared with me about my mother's satisfaction over my change. Some days after her death, a sister told me: "Pastor, while we were listening to you preach on Sunday, your mother said to me:

'Now I can die in peace, my son is a pastor'."

# Anointed to preach

Every time I had an experience — of fear, strife or sadness — that threatened to discourage me from testifying of Christ, the Lord ministered to me in an encounter that lifted me to another dimension.

While walking on a wide street, a strong, tall character appeared behind me in gleaming white clothing. I was not able to remain standing. I fell backwards in the middle of the street. I was motionless. The tall, angelic character stood near my head and commanded: "Open your mouth." My body immediately responded. My mouth opened wide. Then this celestial being took out a great horn, aligned it with my mouth and said: "Drink." A liquid substance, some kind of lubricant, began overflowing from the horn. He held it up with his right hand and, in spite of his great height, not one drop fell out of my mouth as I drank. Then, when I felt full of the thick liquid, he said: "This is the anointing to preach." I drank until the last drop came out of the horn.

# Woe of me if I do not preach the Gospel!

During my mother's funeral, several relatives and friends came to the Lord. Even though I felt pain over my mother's departure, I knew she was in glory. We continued preaching publicly — on radio and even television — and from house to house with great fervor. The church surpassed the average growth rate for New York. Truly, our congregation was not a museum but a fish market. Every service smelled like fish. People out of their own free will came forward and invited Jesus into their hearts. Even more, our church did not simply receive people; we liked to go out and find the lost sheep.

After all, the church was not designed for people to go to it, but for it to go out to the people. "Pastor, there is a mother who is very sad because her son was killed. Can you visit her?" sister Brunilda Bermudez asked. "It's possible there will be more violence. It involved drug dealing. There are also gangs planning revenge."

What a surprise I got when I entered the living room of the house to find thirty young people! Right there, on a not so new sofa, was the suffering mother, crying and sad. Someone had taken her adolescent son's life, along with that of his friend. They both fell into the trap of two girls pretending to love them in order to draw them into their bloody scheme. These young men were ambushed as they entered a building in the Bronx. The first one was stabbed several times; the second one was shot repeatedly. That mother was like Rachel. Who could comfort her? We offered her our sincere support: "Thank you for coming" she said in a sad voice.

One look at the youth group, men and women, and I instantly discerned they were violent, problematic, into the gang lifestyle. Their gestures, appearances and expressions were not strange to me.

In spite of their youth, they already looked like men marked by the streets. The girls also showed such traits. There was no doubt about the kind of life they lived. However, I was not there to condemn them, but to help them. My duty was to present Jesus Christ as Lord. And I did.

# Gang leaders' conversion

Brothers in charge of these and other similar groups worked with fervor until they achieved surprising results.

Groups began converting. In a short time, over fifty gang members began coming regularly to our cell groups. They were delivered in their own homes! All sorts of demons were cast out by the power of the Lord. Demons of witchcraft, drugs and other addictions came out hollering.

We didn't celebrate one worship service without one soul coming to the altar. I felt we were experiencing the Book of Acts. I never experienced a manifestation of both the Spirit of God and of demons as strong as the one that occurred in an upstate camp meeting in New York, where approximately two hundred young people were part of a face-to-face encounter with the forces of darkness.

"Pastor, run. Something terrible is happening on the other side of the lake," yelled a young man pulling me by the arm.

"I bind and rebuke every foul spirit in the name of Jesus!," I shouted, with faith and authority, in the midst of the frantic voices of young people trying to keep some of their peers from throwing themselves into the center of a burning camp fire.

"San Miguel! Archangel San Miguel!" invoked a spirit in a half naked young lady in a high pitched melodic voice, while my wife and other women ministered deliverance to her.

"Here I am! Come Anaisa!," another demon possessed young man called to her.

"Pastor, let me go. Your enemy is behind you. Can't you see him?
Look at him!"

It took us half an hour to take control. We cast out spirits of witchcraft. Many of the young people confessed they had made pacts with spirits of wickedness. Finally, we decided to pray peacefully. Around three o'clock in the morning, when we believed everything was under control, a young man asked to say a word. "I would like to know, why do we pray so much with out mentioning the 'saints?'"

We spent several hours explaining that Jesus is the only begotten Son of God, the Father. We did not mind losing sleep in order to build their foundations in the faith. Soon we began to see results. God allowed the influential gang leaders to come to the Lord first with all of their hearts, bearing true fruits of repentance.

"Many of us believed we would die before the age of eighteen," said Emmanuel, a young maof seventeen years old, former gang leader. Today he is an area coordinator, responsible for six to twelve leaders of cells, each of which has six to twelve disciples.

"Emmanuel died," everybody on the block was saying the day he was stabbed, recalled Maximo "Machi" Guzman, also a former gang leader, now a television producer and area coordinator just like Emmanuel.

"I knew I was being hunted by a group called "Nacion," a big, mean gang," said Emmanuel. "I was caught off guard. Suddenly, a group of them jumped on me at the train stop at 145th and Broadway, on the high side. We began trading punches. They outnumbered us. A stampede began all over the train station.

"All of a sudden, I felt I was being stabbed in the back. Then I felt more stabbing all over my body, especially in the chest and abdomen. 'Are you going to let him die? Take him to the hospital!' a man yelled, while a friend tried to help, stopping the hemorrhage with the wounded boy's handker-

chief. While Machi and the rest were fighting off the surprise attack, returning punches, the atmosphere was very
thick. The women screaming, the men rushing around, and
the sudden flight of the opposing gang confirmed that something besides a normal fight had taken place.

" 'I don't want to die! I don't want to die!' 'Wellington
the Flow' yelled, dressed in multicolored handkerchiefs
wrapped around his head like a turban, while he pretended
to be overtaken by the spirit of Frank, who had been assassinated that same afternoon of September 11th, 1997 while
waiting for the No. 1 train."

A young man fighting for his life was lying in the
Presbyterian Hospital of Manhattan, in Washington
Heights. His companion died after having been stabbed at
the same train stop where he had attacked when his gang
dominated the neighborhood. Such is street life.

"Pastor, I was stabbed, too", said Machi, humorously,
trying to break the tension this account had created in those
listening. "But they had to get me in the back because when
I start running, nobody can catch me."

Not everyone we loved escaped a violent end. Brother
Cortijo, who also came out of Fishkill penitentiary and was
a musician, lost his life when he was caught off guard and
pushed by a schizophrenic brother onto the tracks as a train
was coming at full speed. Although he had left gone to a sister church, we considered him one of us. We feel deeply that
he was taken from the center of our hearts. For those of us
who saw him surrender his heart and grow in the Lord, it
was a devastating experience to say good-bye to him under
these circumstances.

# Wilkins' death

While the guys continued growing in their leadership, God gave them grace to minister in conferences and concerts in the city. Several times they ministered at services where Miguel Cassina, Jaime Murell and Jesus Adrian Romero ministered, among other international worship leaders. People rejoiced hearing the rap groups La Cosecha, directed by Emmanuel Polanco and Los Escogidos, directed by Maximo del Machi Guzman.

Thousands of people, who initially didn't accept this kind of music, were now singing the choruses at our meetings, and clapping their hands with joyful faces.

However, in the middle of victory, the enemy of our souls was planning his most cynical attack: "Pastor, Wilkins has been shot several times! He is in critical condition!", a young man reported with much concern, referring to one of the musicians from La Cosecha, who had several previously fallen back into the world of drug dealing. "They say he is dead. What will we do?" said brother Felix Guzman, while he drove me to St. Luke's Hospital at 114th Street and Amsterdam Avenue in Manhattan.

Felix and his wife Rosa Guzman along with other leaders of the church served as leaders for those young people since their conversion. They lovingly drove them from the cell group meetings to their homes and to every church service. We prayed during the whole trip. When we finally arrived to the hospital, twenty young people received us. Some of them were crying inconsolably; others kept the faith believing that "God would not allow the early departure of an eighteen year old boy".

The doctor gave me the bad news: "Reverend, he died shortly after entering the operating room."

His mother arrived at that time. The tragedy had totally transformed her. She looked like a different woman. It was the 14th of May 2000, Mother's Day.

Although we all suffered, who like her? I gathered all the young people. I asked them to form a circle of prayer. There I gave them the news. The emotional outbreaks were uncontrollable. In front of that hospital, I probably saw the saddest collective experience in my pastorate. To this day, the memory of those tears does not go away. Many young people had questions and doubts, especially during the funeral service at the church: "Pastor, the girls are very nervous. They are anxious. They want to know if Wilkins went to heaven or hell". The answer came from Wilkins' family. His little sister had heard him say, "Father" while bathed in blood close to the sidewalk of 139th Street shot down by four deadly bullets in the head.

In addition, his father stood up in the middle of the service while his son lay in the coffin: "I dreamed that two doves picked my son up in the middle of the street and took him to heaven."

I was able to give a public testimony, in the funeral, of how this young man had an encounter that changed his life. I also mentioned before a church full of hurting people how a member of the Wilkins family, who sold drugs, had challenged several leaders of the church, saying: "You brainwash those young people. They should be looking for money in the streets. And they're wasting time in the church. I swear I'll take all of those kids out of your church, one by one." When I finished my intense message, more than forty young people came to Christ for the first time. Others that had backsliden, reconciled with tears.

# The souls that came to Heavenly Vision church

If you visit our church, don't be surprised if you see a young lady of just seventeen years carrying a newborn baby in her arms. Don't be surprised to see a young man with earrings and long hair; or an adult with scars or tattoos, still smelling like an addict or with a criminal record that doesn't allow him to get a job, a pressure that usually induces him to break the law to find his daily bread or to defend his "macho" reputation.

The police frequently visit our church looking for fugitive convicts, recent crime suspects, probation or parole violators. A minister from another church, when he saw this scenario, criticized our work, accusing us of lacking character and spirituality and operating outside normal church function. My answer to him was that the church is not a museum but a hospital and, a bit disturbed, I added: "Jesus said: 'I will make you fishers of men" (Mathew 4:19).

Brother, I don't have a church but a house full of fishermen."

David, a young man who was in the gangs of "Las Nietas" and "The Zulu Nation", was participating in a fast. He suddenly got the idea that someone was making fun of him during prayer so he ran to the kitchen, took a knife and tried unsuccessfully to harm one of our pastors and two inoffensive young people. Today, he is still in the church. You should see how he weeps during prayer. He doesn't miss a service for anything in the world!

Another man took advantage of the sisters by going through their purses while they were in prayer or worship. Today he is a youth preacher at a church in another county of the city because his parents moved.

Very similar to this case is Sammy Veloz, who visited the chapel of Fishkill penitentiary to dance meringues and salsas, then later became a powerful evangelist in our church. Today, he serves the Lord in Europe.

Another man came to church because the sisters were very pretty, and today he's a great leader. We prepare the leaders of the church not to question the motive of any person that comes to church, but to depend on the transforming power of the Author and Sustainer of the Church, Jesus Christ. It's not about who comes to church, but about Who is in the Church that makes the difference.

Jesus Christ is in our church! Our job is not to convert but to share Jesus Christ. At our church, Jesus is transforming drunkards, addicts, prostitutes, self-righteous, professionals, business people and even religious folks by the power of the Holy Spirit.

This is what Jesus called us to: Win souls, or at the very least, present Him just as He is: Lord and Savior. "Why do so many people die in your church?", asked Michael Ortiz, the president of the Ortiz Funeral Home. "Why do so many convicts go to your church?" others ask. And I find the answer to these questions very simple. Our church should have been named "The New York Soul Factory."

In a factory, not all products come out to the liking of the factory owner. Nevertheless, we cannot stop the work of evangelism due to isolated results, because Jesus has shown his transforming power in homes and public places where many captive souls have been rescued from the steel chains of sin.

We don't care nor do we feel ashamed to visit the courts in supporting of a member of the body who, for a moment, decided to look back. This happens many times. How many times have we visited the hospital to see a member that has fallen victim to violence? We are not ashamed of climbing to a window on an upper storey to rescue a mother that has gone insane and kidnapped her own children. We have run after a backslider until we reached him and hugged him pleading with him to come back to the true way.

We have fought toe to toe with an abusive husband until overcoming him with the unconditional love of the Lord, that shows its power in the church and on the street corners of New York where, when we least expect it, someone raises a hand confessing Jesus Christ as the Son of God.

I am convinced that this work will continue, if not through me, through the lives of others that will rise up in this city, commonly referred to as the modern Babylon. Just as I had so many "puntos" to sell drugs and workers selling drugs in the streets of this city and neighboring states, I will also see this city full of the gospel and the power of the Spirit. The Word of God has begun to diffuse throughout this city. Very soon we will hear through the news anchors, newspaperscolumnists, television channels and the radio: "The City of New York is "full of the knowledge of the Lord, as the waters cover the seas"" (Isaiah 11:9 NIV)

*Two Ways*

# 16
# MIGHTY ACTS

"God has great things for this church," said one prophet after another concerning our congregation. With each prophecy we resolved more deeply to be a people learning to hear God's voice and believe Him with whole hearts. What better way to do this than to praise Him for His mighty acts (Psalm 150:2a) and to begin to pray as Moses did:

"O, Lord God, You have begun to show Your servant Your greatness and Your mighty hand, for what god is there in heaven or on earth who can do anything like your works and your mighty deeds?" (Deuteronomy 3:24)

These words also motivated us to continue pursuing our call. We continued preaching house to house, over radio and television, in the streets and anywhere the Lord sent us.

Three great allies: fasting, prayer and study of the Word

Fasting and prayer were part of our relationship with the Lord early on in our church. It was not unusual to have a brother invite you to join in a fast of several weeks. Rafael Nunez, our head of prison ministry, who had served the Lord with me in Fishkill Penitentiary and had spent more than 15 years in prison, once turned over his house to us so that we could spend 21 days fasting. From September 30 to October 20 of 1996, we were praying and receiving instructions from the Holy Spirit for our church. On Saturday October 19, a group of about 14 men began to pray at six in the morning. We finished at a little after six in the evening. During that time the Lord showed me that the most effective evangelistic strategy for us would be to organize the entire church into cell groups. It had been two years since our church had stopped growinggrown the way it had in the first four years. The reason was that home-based evangelism had been reduced drastically.

The Lord had charged me with studying the book of Acts even before the fast. But I was specially impacted when He pointed out to me the model for the church that is summarized in Acts 5:42: "And daily, in the temple, and in every house, they did not cease teaching and preaching Jesus as the Christ." From this verse was born my first book Koinonia Cells: a strategy for conquering any city for Christ. This book was presented in 1997 to Berean University in order to complete my bachelor'slicensing in Pastoral Theology. In 1989 I had become the first student to graduate from the ministerial studies program in Spanish. In 2001, Scott Harrup, editor of the magazine Pentecostal Evangel, noted that the magazine had been a part of my educational development while I was still behind bars. (Pentecostal Evangel, April 29, 2001, pp. 18-22)

After the fast, all the participants — including nine ex-convicts — laid our hands on the work. The church became infected with a great hunger for souls. In a short time we were 700 in number and still growing. Today we number almost 300 cells that minister in homes to more than 2000 people, 1200 of them members of Heavenly Vision.

## Macoris for Christ

The Lord encouraged us to share the vision with colleagues in ministry. He especially asked us to help anyone who asked for our help. The vision was His, not ours. We obeyed Him. We began to help colleagues in ministry in New York, and other cities in New Jersey, Delaware, Connecticut and Massachusetts  the same areas in which I had dealt drugs  Then he gave me the privilege of returning to the Dominican Republic after 25 years of absence. There I reunited with my brothers and sisters who I loved dearly. I also reconnected with my friends who had been deported. I reconciled sincerely with Forty Seven. I hugged Mike Santos, who I had last seen when we were in jail together. Today he is a pastor, called by the God of heaven. And finally, I could see Ramon el Sweepy Nunez, whom I hadn't seen since the day of our last sentencing. After presenting the Lord Jesus Christ to this dear friend with whom I had shared so much, he suffered a tragic and mysterious death, which took us by surprise, since he had experienced a moral rebirth and had become a successful businessman and the responsible father of a family.

Then the Lord brought to my memory the dream of the young woman weeping bitterly with cries that were heard in all of heaven. I remembered that while I was flying through the air to comfort her, I could see the flat roofs of the houses. Suddenly I recognized that I was passing over the neighborhood of Restauracion of San Pedro de Macoris, where we lived the last part of my childhood. I concluded that the Lord was sending us to take the message to the people of my hometown, the petromacorisanos. The local church received the news with joy. I made contact with my sister, Salvadora "Dorin" Sabino, who served the Lord before me, to put her in charge of helping us in everything that would be necessary.

San Pedro de Macoris, city of two hundred seventy-five thousand inhabitants is popularly known as "the cradle of the great ball players" by virtue of having produced the greatest number of players for the major leagues. More than 70 petromacorisanos have achieved the dream of playing in the Major Leagues. The Pentecostal church, on the other hand, calls it "the cradle of Pentecost" because it was there that a revival, headed by Puerto Rican brothers, was ignited in 1930 and spread through the city by the power of the Holy Spirit.

On Monday, June 20 of 1998, more than 80 intercessors, worshipers and teachers of the Word of God left for the Dominican Republic from New York and New Jersey. They joined with another 100 brothers and sisters from the ministry with which I was serving: Iglesias Crisitianas Fuente de Salvation. (Fount of Salvation Christian Churches) About 80 churches of the Confraternity of Evangelical Churches received us and we went to work, shoulder to shoulder in the conquest of Macoris.

"Macoris for Christ" was a glorious campaign. Approximately 700 disciples met together in First Jerusalem Church every morning for prayer and evangelistic strategies.

In one of the meetings, I took the opportunity to ask forgiveness of Pastor Nestor Nova. "I want to publicly ask forgiveness of this man of God. When I was a child, I used to make fun of him and throw stones at him from my hiding place. There were many nights when we, the troublemaker kids of the neighborhood, would give a concert of stones dropping on the zinc roof to the people gathered in the church for a prayer meeting." The people applauded joyfully when one of the brothers announced that Christ's love had caught one of the "stone throwers."

During the mornings we prayed, shared teachings on

relationship evangelism and motivated each other to share the gospel. Then we spread out through the city in order to give the testimony of Christ in homes, streets, parks and plazas. We visited different institutions: jails, hospitals, children's homes and rehabilitation centers. We gave out clothes, food and money, among other things. We visited various neighborhoods. We visited the sugar mills and, of course, one of those was the Angelina Mill.

While we were kicking up the dust of the main street, dogs, roosters and chickens crossed in front of the bus in which we were traveling. For the first time in a long time, inexplicably, although I said nothing to anyone, a wave of nostalgia overtook me. There could be no doubt that I was a native of that precious little place that had witnessed my birth on Thursday, October 25, 1956 at 4:30 p.m.

That same place almost witnessed my death. I had probably not even yet turned five when my mother came down with a terrible illness. My grandmother, Tata, blamed witchcraft and vowed to take action. "They are going to pay," she said.

I remember clearly as an adult this episode from my infancy, which years later I confirmed. "Drink this milk, papi, come on!" offered my mother, almost forcing me to drink a liquid that looked like cow's milk but smelled much stronger. As she struggled to make me put the glass to my mouth, my grandmother suddenly appeared. "What are you doing, Juanita?" My own mother had tried to poison me. A moment later, a crowd gathered and the screams of my grandmother and the neighbors could be heard along the street. Some men picked up my mother and put her in a car headed for the hospital.

I plunged into a stream of memories, thinking of this

and other bitter events, but like an epiphany, like a sudden revelation, I was filled with joy over my salvation The instant we become aware of the magnitude of the experience of redemption, everything changes. What a great salvation! Then I was able to appreciate the afternoon breeze caressing my face, the blue sky contrasting in the faraway horizon with the green of the leafy tropical trees and the fields of sugar cane. I don't know if this happens to every believer but it was glorious.

The mill by then no longer processed cane. Domingo Sabino, my father, was its last administrator. After his death, the smoke no longer rose from the chimney but you could still hear the "choo choo" of the cargo trains transporting the cane to other centers that were still active. Neither had the place lost the smell of the sugary juice of the cane that spread throughout the factory.

The people, as always, approached the cars curiously to get a look at the visitors. They offered help in installing the sound equipment before we began worship. The people arrived happy, smiling and in groups. Those are the people of Angelina. The service had not been announced, but in less than half an hour we preached to more than two hundred people. "We have come to tell you that Jesus loves Angelina. Jesus loves you. He has not forgotten you."

God did not forget them one year later either when Hurricane George attacked the Dominican Republic with all its fury. The eye of the storm touched San Pedro de Macoris. More than seventy truckloads of supplies arrived due to the efforts of the churches of New York and New Jersey. Our ministry sent two truckloads of almost 40,000 pounds of medicine, food, clothing and furniture. As pastors and missionaries, we gave toward the restoration of the houses of worship. The need in Angelina was so great that in less than half an hour we distributed everything we had brought. They ripped out of our hands the last little thing we were able to give. Our team shed many tears on seeing that, though we had given, we could not sufficiently alleviate the pain of each family.

In the first Angelina crusade, we were in the middle of preaching the word from the top of a truck, when the Holy Spirit moved in. The people fell to the ground under His power. Many were delivered from spirits that left speaking out loud and cursing. In the middle of the excitement, I recognized Nerola, that practitioner of witchcraft who had thrown me to the floor so that I would not see the face of the man who, according to her, had caused the death of papa Rafael. She had also predictedsaid that I would die with my boots on.

"Nerola, save your life. Invite Jesus into your heart," I implored her with a lot of love. Her movements and her fixed gaze evidenced spiritual pain. I discerned that much. Love conquered. "I accept," she said with conviction after a moment. I laid holy hands on her. Suddenly, she fell to the ground while the people applauded with joy that Jesus, in that hour, was the only victor. The next day and the following three nights more than one hundred fifty people of Angelina came to the stadium to participate, as a great family, in the celebration of worship to Jesus Christ.

Wherever we evangelized, we put out a call inviting people to evening services. We gathered twelve thousand people or more in the Tetelo Vargas Stadium, which was shaken by the power of the Holy Spirit for three nights in a row. What a sight! The crowd wrapped up in worship led by the psalmist Jocelyn Arias and our choir, guiding them to the very throne of God!

Apostle Pablo Fernandez and I were in charge of the messages whose central theme was the conquest of the city. We concentrated specifically on sharing the three weapons of conquest and their functions: intercession that binds or paralyzes the enemy (II Kings 19:1-6; Matt. 18-18-20); worship, which confuses the enemy (II Chron.20:20-26); evangelism, which destroys the enemy (Matt. 12:29; Luke 11:21-22.) That is to say, intercession limits the work of the enemy in the city; worship confounds his strategies and, finally, evangelism disposes him of his spoils, which are souls. These messages touched lives and motivated the church to continue preaching the gospel.

The last night was glorious. Before the people of Macoris, more than fifteen thousand of whom were actually present in the service, the mayor, the Honorable Nelson Gums, presented us with a plaque recognizing our work. "Jesus is Lord in San Pedro de Macoris!" he declared. The stadium crowd broke out in exuberant shouts and applause. The following Thursday, July 30, 1998, the newspaper Hoy reported: "As much through the evangelization in the various neighborhoods as during the three nights in the Tetelo Vargas Stadium, some seven thousand souls were converted to Christ.

# New York is declared "City of God"

The evangelistic invasions were frequent. We were serious about the conquest of the conquest of New York for Christ. The motto that we used was "Let us Conquer New York for Christ."

During these activities we would distribute tracts to a whole neighborhood on certain days, while at the same time giving testimony on the street corners and at known drug sale locations, knocking on doors, sharing food with the needy and the young people out for sports events. Finally, we would invite everyone to an evening outdoor service.

On the appointed day, we were having the evening service on Hamilton Place between 137th and 138th streets, after having won close to 500 souls in three days of saturation, when all of sudden a woman dressed in red and black appeared and began doing a dance that was evidently demonic in front of the platform. At that moment the skies darkened and a heavy rain began to fall. I understood that the devil was waging war. He didn't want souls to be saved. I hurried to make the altar call. Fifty souls came to the feet of Jesus underneath a heavy rain even without the power of a microphone!

In a meeting in the offices of Radio Vision Crisitiana (Radio Christian Vision), brother Ruben Greco, a New York publisher, moved by the Holy Spirit while we were planning an activity at the citywide level, declared that " New York is the City of God." This declaration impacted everyone at that meeting. So on October 3, 1998, we gathered about twelve thousand people on Randall's Island, to celebrate "New York, City of God." For people with a prophetic eye, this activity produced a change of environment in our city. For one thing, as the organizers, we enjoyed ourselves exceedingly as we spread out to intercede for the city simultaneously from different locations. Each group of twelve would pray from its spot through RadioVision. From there we all gathered on Randalls Island, while Marcos Witt, the internationally known praise and worship leader, ministered. Everyone was looking up when a flock of geese heading south flew by in V formation. It was highly symbolic for those of us seeking revival for New York. Our least consideration was distinguishing ourselves individually. Rather our desire was to move in a common direction with a true sense of unity in order to accomplish the divine purpose of opening the way for the Lord's perfect will for the city.

But the enemy was not going to let that happen without a fight and he began setting traps with the intent of causing ministerial division in New York. One way or another, he was able to stir criticism, division, and even prolonged enmity, and create an environment of tension that disturbed the blessed cooperation we had been enjoying. There was some unity in facing the trials but we did not emerge completely undamaged.

One of the criticisms against us was that we had become sensationalist. We were questioned: Why did we have to pray around the city in caravans, on bridges, on the tallest skyscrapers and other sites if the Lord could hear us anywhere?

The enemy intensified things with threats of legal action, scandals designed to weaken and split the body. Notwithstanding the fact that the conquest of New York did not reach its culmination, it continued to burn in our hearts with a flame that would not be extinguished.

During a concert, before a congregation of more than three thousand people, the Holy Spirit put in my heart to offer an apple to every leader present and have us eat them in front of the congregation as they supported us in prayer. Each leader came up to the altar to eat his apple while the others prayed that the Lord would be with us while we ate the Big Apple, the city of New York.

# Good News, New York

"Good News, New York" was another similar campaign that had great acceptance despite the obstacles set up by critics and skeptics.

"I never imagined that the leaders of the church of this

city where there are so many souls, would not recognize such a visitation of God," lamented my longtime friend and personal tailor, Genito Mota, on one of the twenty-four nights we traveled to the Good News, New York crusade via the West Side Highway. For six weeks during the summer of 1999, we preached the gospel in the streets of the great city with teams made up of local church members as well as volunteers from several different nations. For twenty-four nights we worshipped and preached Christ from the famous Manhattan arena, Madison Square Garden.

Dr. Rodney Howard Browne, African missionary who had arrived in the United States with only three hundred dollars and his Revival Ministries International, accepted the challenge of investing six and a half million dollars. The Lord allowed me the privilege of serving as the Latin coordinator for "Good News" and also of being present every day and night to win souls for His glory. The second night of the campaign, Thursday July 8, 1999, my dream of sharing my testimony in Madison Square Garden was fulfilled for the first time; then again on Wednesday August 9. I never thought I would so quickly see the fulfillment of one of the dreams I had held in my heart and declared publicly from the altar of the local church. "The nations need to hear that testimony," brother Rodney had told me with a smile. Brother Ben Kinchlow had introduced me with joy, calling out in a lively voice, "This man was a drug dealer in this same city. While he was awaiting his third sentencing, the Lord Jesus Christ visited his cell. Let's listen to the life changing testimony of a former drug dealer, Pastor Sal Sabino."

The Lord gave me the privilege of seeing thousands of people from all sides coming to the feet of Christ. Although more souls were saved in the streets of the city with the evangelistic teams who had come in from different continents, I thoroughly enjoyed watching those touched by Brother Rodney's message run to the altar night after night. I enjoyed it because even though Madison Square Garden is the most famous arena in the world because of its great sporting matches and fantastic shows and concerts, it was now great because it had become a great house of salvation where hundreds surrendered their hearts to Jesus. For us, during this time, Jesus was Lord of Madison Square Garden. During those twenty-four nights, more than forty-eight thousand souls came to the feet of Christ.

Charles Bell, a writer for the Daily News, declared in the Saturday July 10, 1999 edition, p. 20, that we were "saving with a smile." " 'If he can save New York, he can save the world,' said Sabino. 'And I believe that he can save New York,' " Bell concluded his article.

The church with its new name, Heavenly Vision, continued to grow steadily. "The Rev. Sal Sabino, a former drug dealer who has served three prison sentences, is waging a campaign to convert gang members, drug dealers, youth and homeless to his church, which has grown from 120 members to 1,100 in just eight years,'"Reverend Sabino, an ex drug dealer who served three prison sentences, is launching a campaign to convert gangsters, drug dealers, youth and the destitute to his church, which has grown from one hundred and twenty to eleven hundred members in only eight years," noted Christine Haughney in her article "Religion Revives the Bronx," in the national edition of the Washington Post, Sept. 11, 2000.

Various secular and religious media outlets frequently visited us due to our style of evangelism, which attracted people who usually rejected invitations to church. Frequently, reporters were also inquiring about the growth of the Latin churches in the Bronx, which have increased from four hundred to nine hundred in the last five years.

" 'We have begun really practicing evangelism,' said Pastor Hermes Caraballo. ... 'It is a move of the Holy Spirit, a visitation of the glory of God,' said Sabino." So wrote Michael Clark of Christianity.Com, Inc. in his article "A Covenant Made in Heaven," of Sept. 22, 2000.

"In great part, the revival has come as a result of the combination of Pentecostalism and the concentration of Hispanics in the neighborhood. Spirited preachers like Sabino, a native of the Dominican Republic and founder of Heavenly Vision Christian Center, are guiding the growth," added Clark.

The majority of journalists and other media professionals are interested in the fact that many of our members have violent pasts. Of course, I am not offended since I am one of the best examples. What this confirms is nothing more and nothing less than the fact that the power of Christ is at work. There are many who turned over their weapons, revolvers, machine guns, grenades and explosives of every kind after an encounter with Jesus. Imagine the grace of the Lord! A youth on drugs threw himself from the third floor, believing that as he fell perhaps he would sprout wings. However, before crashing onto the concrete sidewalk, he heard the voice of the Lord and converted. Today he serves as an area coordinator in our church, responsible for six to twelve section coordinators, which means he oversees more than one hundred people. This is the impacting story of Mario Junior Pena, whose family serves the Lord after a life of drugs, alcohol and other addictions. How many families has the enemy destroyed in this city? Nevertheless, many have been restored and today serve God in our church.

It is my joy to see evangelist Jose Choco Lazen preach from our altar after losing a career in sports and entering a life of crime that put him in jail for more than ten years. He testifies that he came to Christ by watching my life as we played softball on the same team in the Fishkill Penitentiary. How can I contain the joy I feel on hearing the preaching of our local pastors: Domingo Pino, who wouldn't think twice about picking up a revolver and firing it, and spent years in prison; Ozzie Suarez, who saw so much cocaine pass through his hands; Angel Cuba who, if he hadn't heard the audible voice of God, would have carried out a massacre he was planning using an Uzi and a sawed off shot gun, or Vicente Guzman, a former correctional officer, turned dangerous hoodlum, who now pastors at the Heavenly Vision Christian Center in Long Island

I enjoyed seeing Jenny, a young girl thrown into the street at only ten years of age. She arrived at the church with a cigarette addiction and a husband with whom she traded blows like a man. Her husband tragically lost his life due to an overdose. She did not give up, but fought for her life and her soul. She was later married, covered in honor, to a man of God. Robert and Jenny Pineiro are youth pastors with a prosperous ministry.

I rejoiced in seeing a woman, who we may compare with the Samaritan woman of whom we read in John Chapter 4, now ministering to our neighbors in the Jewish Home in the Bronx. Since we were children, we had been taught: "Those flocks of black birds are the Jews that killed Jesus. And for that they deserve the worst punishment." It was so emphasized that a little friend of mine from childhood pushed a Jewish man and caused him to fall under the wheels of a train at a stop in Washington Heights. Few showed any remorse over this vile action; on the contrary, some justified the act with the above-mentioned false belief.

Thanks be to God, today we have the true revelation even by our own experience. We have been known to cry out at the Western Wall for the restoration of Israel. We love Jerusalem!

Why such a great transformation? In simple words, Jesus has transformed us. Why do we live victorious lives? Simply and only by the filling of the Holy Spirit! The Lord baptizes people in the Holy Spirit in almost all of our meetings, at home and at church. God is doing something new every day in our lives. On one trip to the Holy Land, there in Cana of Galilee, the Lord revealed to me that the new wine that is coming in this time generation will surpass that of His time. Men and women will change the reputation of the city of New York due to the abundance of the Spirit in their lives. It will no longer be known as the modern Babylon but as the city where the grace of God abounds. The people of New York will very soon exclaim, "My cup runs over!" (Psalm 23:5) In order to take a city, it is necessary that you be filled with the Holy Spirit. If you are hungry and thirsty for God, the filling of the Spirit is for you. Jesus said, "If anyone thirsts, let him come to me and drink. He who believes in Me, as the Scripture has said, out of his heart will flow rivers of living water." (John 7:37b-38) Get ready because a great revival is coming!

## The birth of the traveling ministry

Beyond our function as pastors, Kenia and I dedicate ourselves to sharing Jesus through the S.E.A., an acronym for the Sabino Evangelistic Association. We founded this association on June 15, 2000, with a great celebration joined by more than sixty ministers, pastors and bishops from the city and elsewhere, and about 1400 souls. That night we reported that more than 1,200 people came to the feet of the Master during the ten days we had saturated the streets of the Bronx and Washington Heights. Another forty responded after hearing, "Two Ways: The Testimony of an Ex Drug Dealer." That night the success was so great that the idea was born of taking this activity into the schools, auditoriums and stadiums of cities, states and nations wherever the Holy Spirit would send us.

After the inauguration of the SEA, we launched a coast-to-coast evangelistic tour through the United States, as well as Puerto Rico and the Dominican Republic. We were pleased to be part of the move of God in different cities and nations. On June 20, 2000, I had the privilege of giving the testimony "Two Ways" on the opening night of "Good News, America" in the Hirsh Coliseum at Shreveport, Louisiana, another six-week evangelistic invasion sponsored by Revival Ministries International where more than fifty-thousand people came to Christ. Although we go out frequently with the gospel of Jesus Christ, we try to be in our local church, Heavenly Vision, every weekend.

# The Lord changed the course of my destiny by His grace

The Lord took me by His powerful hand from the street, drugs, crime and prison. He visited me in a prison cell where it seemed I had no hope. He showed me the true path by His grace. After all, what did I deserve but the worst punishment? He gave me the opportunity to follow Him. I chose to follow Him with my whole heart. My joy now is to serve Him. I rejoice in preaching His Word, writing books such as Koinonia Cells: an evangelistic strategy for conquering any city for Christ and The Second Anointing, which proves through Scripture that it is possible to rise to a higher dimension of anointing every day. I also rejoice in having written hymns such as "The Throne

Sublime," "Your Glory," "Oh, Spirit," "Instrument of War," among others that have been recorded by the Lord's psalmist, Jocelyn Arias, who is also a product of what God is doing with the people of Washington Heights. She walked in the world of traveling pop artists for more than 20 years singing with the group "Millie, Jocelyn y Los Vecinos," but today she is an ambassador of song in the name of our Lord Jesus Christ.

Of course, nothing that I have done could pay for what He has done for me. Through Him, I have life; for Him, I want to live.

A list of those who, along with me, drew guns during their lives in the streets would prove, without a doubt, that most of them were either killed or incapacitated, or are still in prison serving long sentences. Through the Lord Jesus I am alive, for Him I want to live.

## Back in Washinton Heights

I wanted to do everything He required of me. Recently, he sent me to a new area of Washington Heights, in Manhattan, exactly where I had lived so much of my life of crime. I knocked on as many doors as possible, looking for a place to hold worship. We spoke with pastors, asking them to let us use space in their churches during any hour they were not in session themselves. We told them we had a great harvest of souls we did not want to lose.

Meanwhile, the cells continued growing. When we reached the point of frustration, the Lord caused us to begin praying without ceasing. I spent long hours together with Rafael Rodriguez, who today is my assistant pastor in the Manhattan congregation. We went all around the island of Manhattan by car, by train, on foot, praying for many months. Not one door opened.

"Lord, if you grant that my friend Henry would be the pianist of this new church, I will believe that that is the sign that will confirm you are opening a door in Manhattan," I prayed one morning, after ministering to the family of Henry Tineo, one of the musicians in a group from our youth.

Finally we visited the largest auditorium in Washington Heights and the third largest of its kindbiggest in New York City, the United Palace Theater. As soon as we entered the auditorium, I declared, full of faith, "We will worship the Lord in this place, in the name of Jesus." Some tried to put us off, saying, "You'll never get into that place. It's too expensive. No Latin church could pay that kind of rent. Besides, the owner doesn't share that place with anybody."

The owner of the theater, Rev. Frederick Eikerenkoetter, possibly the richest minister in the world, who visited the place maybe once a year, was on a visit to New York and wanted to meet me, since a young person from his team had told him how the Lord had transformed me. After passing through a rigorous security system, I was finally escorted to meet him. He was seated in an armchair that bore the design of a crown directly over his head. His two bodyguards, one on each side and his impeccable personal appearance evidenced that he was living like a king in Hollywood. He stood to his feet and, breaking into laughter, he hugged me and said, " So you are Pastor Sabino. I have been believingasking God to raise up someone who wanted to do something in Washington Heights. You are a missionary in Washington Heights. Did you know that?" – he said, still laughing with remarkable courtesy.

"Thank you," I answered, with a touch of nervousness.

"I was a poor boy, fourteen years old, the only preacher in the whole school. But I didn't have the money to buy a sandwich like the others. On more than one occasion, I pawned my coat just so I could go to school. For that, I challenged God. I told him: Lord, if you don't give me sandwich money for tomorrow, I will not preach your word any more. I've never been hungry since," he testified, maintaining the smile of a wise man. "I see hunger in you. That's how I filled packed Madison Square Garden in 1971. I believe you'll do it, too. You've got faith. Tell me about yourself," Reverend Ike asked me. And I shared with him a great part of my testimony, to which he listened with interest and without interruptions.

What a great privilege God has given me! He brought me back as an ambassador of Christ, as a preacher, to the neighborhood where I was a delinquent. How many crimes had I committed in this community? I remember on one occasion, about twenty years earlier, I ran past the United Palace at 175th Street and Broadway, pistol in hand, to do away with an alleged offender. I went back to visit, attracted by the reverend's Rolls Royces. I came out of admiration for the money. Only the Lord, by his grace, could have changed all that! Today, from the United Palace Theater, located at that same corner, I preach that Jesus Christ is coming to proclaim liberty to the captives. (Luke 4:18d) What a great privilege it is to see souls coming into that theater, especially those that come from the streets, lifting holy hands, giving praise to their Deliverer. What a privilege it is to hear their testimonies of how the Lord took them out of the gangs, the violence, drugs, prostitution, witchcraft, among other perversions! More than a regular church, Heavenly Vision is a refuge. "The United Palace serves as a house for Christ United Church and Heavenly Vision Christian Center", wrote New York Times reporter David Dunlop, in the weekend edition of April 13, 2001 (p. E34)

Although my wife and I founded the evangelistic association, The SEA, and we travel throughout the United States and other nations carrying the message, our highest joy is to see what has begun to happen in Washington Heights, in the Bronx and in many other parts of the city of New York. Something great will happen concerning the kingdom of God in New York that will have a worldwide impact as has happened with other aspects of this city. We declare with full conviction that God is at the point of shaking this city with the power of his Spirit.

# I was not disobedient to the "Heavenly Vision"

The Holy Spirit comes on the believer with the purpose of giving him the power to become a witness and carry out His plan for local evangelism with a global vision. Heavenly Vision received a divine charge not to be disobedient to the Heavenly Vision.. (Acts 26:19) The church of our time has to be in constant mobilization for the sake of the salvation of souls.

"Go" is the supreme call to action in all the Bible. (Matthew 28:19; Mark 16:15 and Acts 1:8) Jesus Christ died for souls. We are fulfilling the plan that God gave us for visiting every house and evangelizing publicly, first in the two areas where we are located and then through each area of the city of New York. We have the goal of winning more than thirty thousand souls for Christ in the in the next five months, by preaching the Word in a coherent manner, both in public and house to house. (Acts 20:20)

Our cell groups are leading others to a saving knowledge of Christ in homes on their official meeting days. They are also going from building to building. After every

Sunday service, we go out in the power of the Spirit to preach and teach Christ publicly and from house to house.in houses and in the streets. Then on the other days, especially on selected Saturdays, we preach along avenues and at strategic points in teams of three to six and, finally, we close out each month with a three-day crusade, During our last crusade of the summer we pray by air, sea and land. We make a trip around the island of Manhattan by ferry with five hundred thirty-five prayer warriors and a boat full of believers. Leaders will usually go up in helicopters and, simultaneously, hundreds of cars and motorcycles will take a trip around the island. Then we launch into the streets to preach the grace of Jesus Christ over the city in an evangelistic invasion with several churches participating. Finally, we get together in a centrally located park in order to worship Jesus, the Lord of New York City.

The newspapers and other media will declare: "Thousands convert to Christ and proclaim with one voice: New York, city of God! New York, city of God!"

# Vision of the last days

The coming of the Lord is near. I had a vision in which I was in the center where the four cardinal points of the earth are joined. Suddenly, I saw that the sun, the stars and other heavenly bodies stopped shining. I felt frightfully dangerous vibrations. I looked toward the East and noted that the horizon was advancing with the impetus of a raging fire that covered the entire Orient. I tried to escape toward the West. But another wave of fire was advancing with equal force from that direction. Then I wanted to escape toward the South. Another torrent of fire was advancing in the same way. The glow of the fire allowed me to observe how humanity was alarmed; how people were running in every direction looking for mercy, help and comfort. In that race to the death, the strong trampled and ran over the weak. Nobody wanted to help anyone else, nor were they even able to. Nobody was helping women, or the elderly or the invalids or the newborn. It was horrific! Everyone was screaming.

Large and small lamented: "Aaaaaah! The world is ending! The end has come!" It was as if mercy, help and comfort had disappeared from the earth. It was horrible!

The streets of the cities, large and small were bathed in the blood flowing from their children. With each passing second the pain and screaming intensified. When the scene was at its most difficult, I also thought like the others – only of myself. So I too trampled and ran over people, looking in desperation to escape the terrible judgment. Finally, I ran toward the north, but from there too came a great fire speeding down over the earth. There was no escape eastward. There was no escape westward, nor one to the south, neither to the north. But something unexpected happened. I thought I was going to die, but the Lord changed the course of my destiny in that vision, as he had in my life.

I identify with the psalmist who said: "The voice of rejoicing and salvation is in the tents of the righteous; the right hand of the Lord does valiantly. The right hand of the Lord is exalted; the right hand of the Lord does valiantly. I shall not die, but live, And declare the works of the Lord." (Psalm 118:15-17)

As an oasis appears in the desert, so appeared a crystal river in the Northeast. This river was, I believe, visible to everyone. However, not everyone ran toward it. It seemed that the majority did not believe that river would bring them relief. The majority did not believe that river would bring them salvation.

For my part, I saw no other alternative. Before me, I saw two ways: one was the river of salvation; the other, the fire of judgment. While I was running, out of breath, at top speed toward the river, I discerned that at the river there certainly was mercy, help and comfort. That river was the grace of God. That river was Jesus. As soon as I submerged myself in the river, I could see others diving in as well. The waters were refreshing. The currents carried us quickly away from the burning fire. The more we swam, the more we were filled with joy. As we moved into the deep waters of that crystal river, we gave thanks. We sang, with jubilance, the heavenly chorus: "We are saved, thanks to Jesus, we are saved."

That river from the northeast is the river of God, the very same one that will soon inundate the Northeast of the United States, including New York. Not long ago, the Lord showed me the people of New York swimming in that river of refreshing, abundant, crystal clear water. Men, women, youths and children, people of every race and denomination were swimming together. Nobody complained about racial differences, social status or doctrinal preference.differences.

Everyone recognized Jesus as the Lord of lords. We were full of joy. In the middle of that river or joy, I heard a heavenly voice saying to me: "Tell my people that's how they will swim in my revival" Glory to God in the highest! Come on, God is calling you! Say yes to eternal life! Reserve your seat on the celestial flight! Declare him your Lord and be an active soldier in His kingdom! Follow Jesus.

*"I am the way, the truth and the life; no one comes to the Father, but by Me,"* said the Lord. Jesus is the true way. Follow Him!